T0206801

Cambridge Elements ≡

Elements in Evolutionary Economics
edited by
John Foster
University of Queensland
Jason Potts
RMIT University
Isabel Almudi
University of Zaragoza
Francisco Fatas-Villafranca
University of Zaragoza
David A. Harper
New York University

EXPLAINING TECHNOLOGY

Roger Koppl
Syracuse University
Roberto Cazzolla Gatti
University of Bologna
Abigail Devereaux
Wichita State University
Brian D. Fath
Towson University
James Herriot
Herriot Research
Wim Hordijk
SmartAnalytiX
Stuart Kauffman
Institute for Systems Biology
Robert E. Ulanowicz
University of Florida
Sergi Valverde
Spanish National Research Council

CAMBRIDGE
UNIVERSITY PRESS

Shaftesbury Road, Cambridge CB2 8EA, United Kingdom

One Liberty Plaza, 20th Floor, New York, NY 10006, USA

477 Williamstown Road, Port Melbourne, VIC 3207, Australia

314–321, 3rd Floor, Plot 3, Splendor Forum, Jasola District Centre, New Delhi – 110025, India

103 Penang Road, #05–06/07, Visioncrest Commercial, Singapore 238467

Cambridge University Press is part of Cambridge University Press & Assessment, a department of the University of Cambridge.

We share the University's mission to contribute to society through the pursuit of education, learning and research at the highest international levels of excellence.

www.cambridge.org
Information on this title: www.cambridge.org/9781009386258

DOI: 10.1017/9781009386289

First published 2023

A catalogue record for this publication is available from the British Library.

ISBN 978-1-009-38625-8 Paperback
ISSN 2514-3573 (online)
ISSN 2514-3581 (print)

Explaining Technology

Elements in Evolutionary Economics

DOI: 10.1017/9781009386289
First published online: August 2023

Roger Koppl
Syracuse University

Roberto Cazzolla Gatti
University of Bologna

Abigail Devereaux
Wichita State University

Brian D. Fath
Towson University

James Herriot
Herriot Research

Wim Hordijk
SmartAnalytiX

Stuart Kauffman
Institute for Systems Biology

Robert E. Ulanowicz
University of Florida

Sergi Valverde
Spanish National Research Council

Author for correspondence: Roger Koppl, rkoppl@syr.edu

Abstract: A long tradition explains technological change as recombination. Within this tradition, this Element develops an innovative combinatorial model of technological change and tests it with 2,000 years of global GDP data and with data from US patents filed between 1835 and 2010. The model explains (1) the pace of technological change for a least the past two millennia, (2) patent citations, and (3) the increasing complexity of tools over time. It shows that combining and modifying preexisting goods to produce new goods generates the observed historical pattern of technological change. A long period of stasis was followed by sudden superexponential growth in the number of goods. In this model, the sudden explosion of about 250 years ago is a combinatorial explosion that was a long time in coming but inevitable once the process began at least two thousand years ago. This Element models the Industrial Revolution as a combinatorial explosion.

Keywords: economic growth, combinatorial evolution, economic niche emergence, Industrial Revolution, adjacent possible

JEL codes: A10, E00, E14, O00, O30

ISBNs: 9781009386258 (PB), 9781009386289 (OC)
ISSNs: 2514-3573 (online), 2514-3581 (print)

Contents

1 Introduction

The first knapped stone tools seem to have been created by *Australopithecus afarensis* about 3.3 million years ago (Harmand et al. 2015) and thus before the emergence of genus *Homo* about 2.8 million years ago (Villmoare et al. 2015). *Homo sapiens* seem to have emerged less than about 315,000 years ago (Hublin et al. 2017, Schlebusch et al. 2017). Thus, the history of technology is more than ten times longer than the history of biologically modern humans. It is longer by an order of magnitude. (See the Appendix for details.) An integrated view of this long history of technology requires a broadly Darwinian perspective.

It matters that mRNA vaccines, voice-recognition software, double-entry bookkeeping, positional notation, Roman aqueducts, bronze, and Paleolithic hand axes all share a common evolutionary history with the stone tools of our australopithecine forebears. Even Renaissance art (Wreschner et al. 1980, Singels and Schoville 2018) and rock music (Smith 2020, Smith et al. 2021) participate in and emerged from this common evolutionary history. The long evolutionary history of technology has shaped our brains and bodies. For example, humans are "biologically committed to a diet of cooked food" (Wrangham and Carmody 2010, p. 189) and we have "greater manipulative ability" with our hands than do other modern apes (Panger et al. 2002, p. 238). Technology has done as much to shape humans as humans have done to shape technology (Henrich 2016). Any explanation of technology should be consistent with this coevolution of humans and technology. Combinatorial explanations may have greater potential than their rivals to fit this coevolution comfortably.

If the combinatorial evolution of technology precedes the emergence of biologically modern humans, our explanation of it should be as much "biology" as "economics." In other words, we should adopt a zoological perspective on the evolution of technology. We develop such an explanation, considering rival explanations and placing our explanation in the context of "The zoological perspective in social science" (Tiger and Fox 1966). (See Koppl 2021 for a discussion of the zoological perspective, which he construes broadly.) Our explanation owes much to Brian Arthur's (2009) theory of "combinatorial evolution." We contribute a novel mathematical model of combinatorial evolution and a novel theory of the emergence of economic niches.

Our mathematical model of combinatorial evolution explains the historical increase in global cambiodiversity (variety in the goods produced), including the sudden explosive increase of the Industrial Revolution. This exuberant ramification in output implies a similar exuberant ramification in economic niches, which are potential markets for goods. As far as we know, the economics literature contains no satisfactory account of this ramifying niche emergence, which is a significant omission. Building on Cazzolla Gatti (2011) and related works, we develop such a theory in Section 6.

Our novel mathematical model of combinatorial evolution has at least three very different empirical implications, which we develop below in Section 5.

First, our model predicts the "hockey stick of economic growth," whereby a very long period of low average incomes was followed by sudden super-exponential growth beginning about 1800 CE. (Mokyr 2005 seems to be the first work to have imported the hockey-stick simile from climate science to economics.) Using data from the last two thousand years, we fit a simplified growth model that incorporates our model and gets a good fit.

Second, our model explains an observed power law of the descendant distribution in patent citations. A patent must cite the earlier patents it builds on. Thus, we can ask how many descendants a given patent has – how many children, grandchildren, great-grandchildren, and so on. Our model predicts a power law in this descent distribution. Using US patent data from 1835 to 2010, we find the predicted descent distribution. As explained in this Element, the measured power-law coefficient of −1.30 falls within the range of likely values (−1.1 to −1.35) suggested independently by Steel, Hordijk, and Kauffman (2020) in simulations that, in turn, seem consistent with our growth model. Thus, we are reinforced in the subjective feeling that we are carving nature at the joints.

Third, our model explains the increasing complexity of goods over time, measured by the number of components per good. If goods multiply by recombination, the number of components ("techno-units") in the most complex good in the system will rise. Unfortunately, we cannot give this prediction as strong or clear an empirical test as our other two results. The scant evidence available to us, however, seems to be fully consistent with this prediction of our model.

Three distinct implications of our model fit the available data. We thus have what might be called a "tri-data result." Salient and important patterns in three very different sorts of data covering different segments of time and space are all explained by one simple model. We view this tri-data result as strong evidence for both Arthur's general theory of the combinatorial evolution of technology and our specific mathematical model thereof.

We are proposing an evolutionary theory of technology. It is always possible, of course, to say that technology "evolves." But this statement does not give us a *mechanism* of evolution. Little progress is made by invoking the holy trinity of variation, selection, and retention. Certainly, Darwinian evolution has variation, selection, and retention, as Campbell (1965), Nelson and Winter (1982),

Hodgson and Knudsen (2010), and many others have explained.[1] This trinity rightly affirms the *fact* of variation, but it does not tell us *how* variations occur. It does not explain the "arrival of the fittest" (Schurman 1887, p. 78). Following Kauffman (1988), Arthur and Polak (2006), Arthur (2007, 2009), and many others, we explain the arrival of the fittest with combination. "That is, technological advances often recombine parts from many different machines or products to form a new product" (Kauffman 1988, p. 140). Genius, search, chance, and error play their roles, but recombination is the essential driver of technological evolution. Science, institutions, and culture are, perhaps, moderating factors along the way, but recombination is the essential driver of technological evolution (Solé et al. 2016).

We should have a broad notion of what is being combined in the combinatorial evolution of technology. Schumpeter (1911 [1934], p. 15) spoke of combining "things and forces." If we consider only combinations of things and forces, then the theory might not apply to the earliest stages of technological evolution; it might not apply until after composite tools kicked in about 500,000 years ago (Wilkins et al. 2012). Composite tools are "conjunctions of at least three techno-units, involving the assembly of a handle or shaft, a stone insert, and binding materials" (Ambrose 2001, p. 1751). The term "techno-unit" was coined by Oswalt (1976, p. 38). He says, "In general terms technounits are all the different kinds of parts that make up an artifact. A more exacting definition is that *a technounit is an integrated, physically distinct and unique structural configuration that contributes to the form of a finished artefact*" (Oswalt 1976, p. 38, emphasis in original). The earliest composite tools seem to be spears made by affixing ("hafting") a sharp stone point to a wooden shaft (Wilkins et al. 2012). Their makers *combined* existing tools to produce new tools.

If we include human actions among the "things" being combined in the evolution of the technosphere, the theory of combinatorial evolution probably applies to the complete history of technology from the first appearance of knapped stone tools 3.3 million years ago. Read and Andersson (2019) explain a sense in which we may say that a hand axe made by *Homo erectus* is "more complex" than a chimpanzee termite stick, even though each tool has only one piece. The structure of relations among the actions required to make the hand

---

[1] Hodgson and Knudsen (2010) prefer the term "replication" to "retention." They are careful to give the term a precise meaning that requires us to clearly distinguish the "interactors," such as organisms, from the "replicators," such as genomes, that interactors host. The word "retention," by contrast, often gets a looser and fuzzier meaning to the effect that traits are somehow passed along. As Aldrich et al. (2008, p. 587) and Hodgson and Knudsen (2010) have pointed out, this loose meaning makes it hard to distinguish inheritance from contagion.

axe is more elaborate, having a relatively rich array of hierarchically nested goals (pp. 9–12).[2]

We are not interested in all combinations of goods, objects, forces, and actions. As Arthur notes, the "most basic" meaning of "technology" is "a means to fulfill a human purpose" (2009, p. 28). (It is too cumbersome to speak of *classes* of means and *classes* of human purposes, though in strict logic we should.) Arthur also includes in the meaning of "technology" both "an assemblage of practices and components" and "the entire collection of devices and engineering practices available to a culture." We concur with these definitions of technology, at least if "engineering practices" is given a meaning broad enough to include the prehuman knapping of stone tools. We would only add the requirement that the goods, combinations, devices, and practices that we call "technology" be reproducible. For our purposes, it is not "technology" if a broken bit of soup bone happens to work as a door stop. That improvised means to an end is not reproducible. Such broken bone bits would be "technology" only if they were being regularly produced for use as door stops. A technology is a reproducible means to an end.

Our general approach to technology and economic evolution has affinities with some recent work in both complexity economics and evolutionary economics. Without pretending to give a thorough review, we mention a few salient examples.

Complexity economist Eric Beinhocker (2006, pp. 244 and 247) notes the "combinatorial property" of "physical technologies." Citing Arthur (2009) and others, Beinhocker (2011) says, "Novelty clearly comes from the recombinative process of evolutionary search in design space" (p. 415). We make a similar claim (also in the context of Arthur 2009), but without viewing evolutionary search as algorithmic. We follow Hidalgo et al. (2007) in associating cambio-diversity with wealth. Our general perspective, including our recombinant growth model, is close to that of Weitzman (1998), Hausmann and Hidalgo (2011), and Hausmann et al. (2013). Hausmann and Hidalgo (2011, p. 315) say, "When it comes to growth theory, our approach is related to the recombinant growth model introduced by Weitzman (1998), which is in itself highly related

---

[2] This statement simplifies their analysis. They scrupulously note that "it is hard to define precisely what we mean by complexity of a system" (p. 8). Complexity may be undecidable in the same sense that da Costa and Doria (1991) have shown chaos to be undecidable. "There is no general algorithm to distinguish between chaotic and non-chaotic systems, for any reasonable definition of chaos" (Chaitin, da Costa, and Doria 2012, p. 92). We do not know of any proof that complexity is also undecidable. It is reasonable to conjecture, however, that it is. It may be inevitable, therefore, that the sort of complexity comparisons Read and Anderson (2019) attempt will often require relatively lengthy and detailed discussions and close attention to idiosyncrasies of the relevant phenomena.

to the grammar model introduced by Kauffman (1993). In both, Weitzman's and Kauffman's models, the development of new varieties emerges as combinations of previous varieties."

Evolutionary economists Silverberg and Verspagen (2005) say, "Agents tend to search locally for new technologies, i.e., they try combinations and extensions of existing knowledge close in some space of technological characteristics to what they already know and use" (p. 227). Witt (2009) hypothesizes that the first stage in the "creation of new cognitive concepts" is "a generative operation that produces new (re-)combinations of elements" (p. 313).

We think combination is the key mechanism of innovation and technological evolution. And in this Element we will give some reasons to prefer it to rivals such as genius. But we do not pretend to demand that every model of innovation or technological change put our preferred mechanism at the center. Different models serve different purposes. Evolutionary economists Almudi and Fatas-Villafranca (2021), for example, show how, in "contemporary capitalist economies" (p. 66), the "innovative capacity of an upstream-production sector can be constrained by the absorptive capacity of the downstream-user sector" (p. 1). This purpose is different from our purpose in this Element. Given their different analytical context, it is reasonable and appropriate for Almudi and Fatas-Villafranca to view innovation (roughly) as a random draw from a Pareto distribution (p. 15). More generally, different models serve different purposes and may well employ, therefore, different modeling strategies. Thus, the absence from our review of any attempt to assess the evolutionary economics literature since, say, Nelson and Winter (1982) does not mean that we reject or disparage contributions to this literature.

2 Competing Explanations of Technology

There can be no complete or definitive list of explanations of technology, but we think it helpful to discuss several broad categories that have appeared in the literature in different ways.

Genius

The most obvious and naïve explanation of technology may be solitary genius. Technological change is a matter of ideas, and ideas are inexplicable gifts born from the brow of genius. This is probably the most common theory outside academia. It is implicitly invoked by countless books, stories, movies, and television shows featuring figures such as the solitary genius or mad scientist. ("It's alive!" cries Dr. Frankenstein, "It's alive!") Muthukrishna and Henrich (2016) equate the view that "innovation is an individual endeavour, driven by heroic geniuses and then passed on to the masses" with "folk-historical" stories of "savvy ancestors" such as Prometheus who discovered knowledge that was then "passed down from generation to generation." This sort of theory has some very sophisticated advocates as well. George Shackle emphasized the subjective and ex nihilo character of "choosables," which suggests that technological change is driven by the inexplicable arrival of new ideas. He says that "choosables" are *"originated by the chooser"* and thus have "the quality of a *beginning"* in his "extreme sense, the new existence of something not ascribable to antecedents" (Shackle 1979, p. 23, emphases in original).[3] Alvarez, Barney, and Anderson (2013, p. 308) have something similar in mind when they describe "created opportunities" as "social constructions that do not exist independently of those perceptions and human action."

Alvarez, Barney, and Anderson and G. L. S. Shackle recognize that ex nihilo creative ideas must be tested against reality. They nevertheless view the origin or arrival of such ideas as fundamentally inexplicable. But if technology advances by the inexplicable arrival of new ideas, then any "explanation" of it would be limited in scope and power.

Search

Modern growth theorists in economics often view technology as a product of "ideas," and "ideas" as a product of search (Romer 1990, Galor and Weil 2000, p. 816). The word "search" has many meanings, and R&D matters in modern economies. But an explanation of technology on the timescales we are considering should not assume a level of rational, deliberative calculation that is more characteristic of modern "capitalism" (Weber 1927) than of prehistoric humans or even of medieval merchants such as Marco Polo. Nor should we impute modern cognitive prowess to earlier species or variants.

If the combinatorial evolution of technology can be traced back to the emergence of composite tools 500,000 years ago, then the process was in place with *Homo heidelbergensis* (Wilkins et al. 2012) whose brain size seems to have been about 8 percent smaller than that of modern *Homo sapiens* (Melchionna et al. 2020, supplementary information). And if the combinatorial evolution of technology can be traced back to the first knapped stone tools 3.3 million years ago, then the process was in place with *Australopithecus afarensis* (Harmand et al. 2015), whose brain size seems to have been about 68 percent smaller than that of modern *Homo sapiens* (Melchionna et al. 2020,

---

[3] We will later vindicate to some degree Shackle's emphasis on "imagination." But, we will insist, "imagination" combines preexisting elements and is thus not a "beginning" in Shackle's extreme sense.

supplementary information). It is implausible to impute full economic rationality to such relatively small-brained creatures.

Modeling early toolmakers as investing in R&D or human capital or as using "knowledge and human capital ... to produce new designs or knowledge" (Romer 1990, p. S80) would be appropriate only as an "as if" modeling technique. Evolutionary pressures produce the same result "as if" our prehistoric ancestors were making a rational calculation of how much to invest in "ideas." But as-if models leave unanswered the question of mechanism (Nelson and Winter 1982, p. 141). For our purposes in this Element, it does not matter whether the as-if rationality of standard economic growth models does or does not "work." If we are to explain technology, we need to identify the mechanisms driving technological evolution, which as-if theorizing cannot do. Weitzman (1998) was probably right to complain that the "production function for new knowledge" in this literature is a "black box" that could profitably be replaced with a "combinatoric" model (p. 332). While our purposes extend beyond modern growth theory, we believe our combinatoric model can contribute to this literature by offering a more satisfactory model of technological change.

Science, Culture, and Institutions

Science cannot "explain technology" because we had technology before we had science. Nor can we explain technology with "culture" or "institutions." Humans and australopithecines were always social animals and thus always had something like culture or institutions governing their interactions. But the "institutions" of our biological ancestors were endogenous to the coevolution of genes, culture, and technology. More modern institutions such as British common law are also endogenous on sufficiently long views. Empires and legal regimes come and go, but the combinatorial evolution of technology goes back at least 500,000 years when composite tools emerged, and likely 3.3 million years ago with the first knapped stone tools.

Boyd and Richerson (1985), Henrich (2016), and others have drawn our attention forcefully to the coevolution of genes and culture. And biological evolution has shaped human psychology, as emphasized in the rather different tradition of Barkow et al. (1992). In what follows we echo Nelson and Nelson's (2002, p. 725) call for "setting human knowledge" into a "biological evolutionary framework."

Chance and Error

If time and chance happeneth to them all, luck and error must contribute to technological evolution. Arthur (2009, pp. 103, 105, 199) notes that chance always plays a role. Whatever the role of luck in determining relative performance, it is an insufficient explanation of the global pace of technological change over decades, centuries, and millennia. Attributing novelty to "chance" is no explanation at all. It may be more plausible to attribute novelty to "error." Like chance, error surely plays a role. But we do not believe that the evolution of the technosphere has been just one damn thing after another, just one massive cluster of errors. Any such theory is unable to explain how technology ramifies over time to give us increasing numbers of goods and increasing complexity of goods. Boyd, Richerson, and Henrich (2013, p. 139) believe "errors will usually degrade complex adaptive traits."

The positive role of chance and error in the evolution of technology is in generating new combinations.[4] Fleming's chance discovery of penicillin and its good effects (Fleming 1929) illustrates. This discovery may be the most clichéd example of an innovation through chance or error. But the path from Fleming's lab to a usable drug owes less to chance than the standard story allows. It was a difficult problem to purify penicillin without destroying its antibacterial effects, and the problem was not cracked until about 1940 (Howie 1986, p. 158). The technological advance did not consist in noticing that mold spores are effective against bacteria. Citing Lax (2005) and Clark (1985), Arthur (2007, p. 281) says, "others had noted the phenomenon before him – John Tyndall in 1876 and André Gratia in the 1920s, for example." Tullock imagines, "The same accident must have happened to hundreds of other researchers" (1966, p. 9). The technological advance, instead, was in finding the right *combination* of technological elements to reliably purify penicillin and deliver it to sick persons.

Nelson (2008, p. 88) says, "Here the original discovery of the antibiotic properties of the mold was done by one person, Fleming. The experimental work on using the substance as a treatment for infection was done by someone else, Florey and colleagues. And the development of an effective production method was done by still other people."

The invention of Post-it notes is often represented as a mistake, error, or failure that was then recognized to have an unintended beneficial property. Petroski (1992) reports, however, that this supposed mistake was turned into Post-it notes only because of 3M employee Art Fry's willful search for "sticky bookmarks that could be removed without damaging the book" (p. 84). In both famous cases, penicillin and Post-it notes, chance had indeed produced something that was neither sought after nor expected. But in both cases the discoverer was alert to the possibilities. As Muthukrishna and Henrich (2016) note, chance discoveries depend on "a mind prepared to recognize the discovery embedded

---

[4] This claim follows from Arthur's (2009) first principle of combinatorial evolution, discussed later in this Element, that "technologies, all technologies, are combinations."

in chance observation." Fry wanted to solve the problem of bookmarks that slip out of the book. Until he had acquired that interest, the "unglue" he knew of as a 3M employee had no meaning to him. Luck similarly favored Fleming's prepared mind.

For both penicillin and Post-it notes, a chance event could become an innovation only because of an interest or orientation of the discoverer. It was this interest that gave the chance event meaning. Thus, there was a sort of predisposition to notice the opportunity at hand. In Section 5 we discuss this predisposition in connection with "Homo tinkerus" and Israel Kirzner's (1973) theory of entrepreneurial discovery.

Imitation

Boyd and Richerson (1985), Henrich (2016), and others have put forward a theory of gene–culture coevolution in which cultural evolution and, therefore, technological evolution are driven by imitation. Henrich (2016) reviews evidence that our bodies are dependent on technological innovations that are not instinctual. Modern humans have no instinct for the control or ignition of fire, and yet our puny intestines, unsatisfactory jaw muscles, and small mouths make us dependent on cooking to survive (Henrich 2016, pp. 65–69). These facts about our anatomy help to make their general idea of gene–culture coevolution persuasive. But imitation might seem an unlikely source of novelty. If an evolutionary model has variation, selection, and retention, then imitation might seem to be strongest on retention and weakest on variation. But Boyd, Richerson, and Henrich (2013, p. 137) have said, "By recombining different components of technology from different, but still successful individuals, copiers can produce both novel and increasingly adaptive tools and techniques over generations without any improvisational insights." Without this link to recombination, it might be hard to associate imitation to innovation.

Given the link to recombination, "imitation" does have explanatory power. Boyd and Richerson (1985), Boyd, Richerson, and Henrich (2013), and Henrich (2016) neglect or minimize the role of recombination in cultural evolution. Muthukrishna and Henrich (2016), however, give it more extensive treatment. They say, "the three main sources of innovation are serendipity, recombination and incremental improvement." Muthukrishna and Henrich (2016) underestimate path dependency and nonergodicity in cultural and technological evolution when they say, "Potential innovators, exposed to the same cultural elements, arrive upon the same discoveries, in their own minds, independently; but from the perspective of the collective brain, these ideas are spreading and will eventually meet, unless they are forgotten first." Our model of combinatorial evolution implies that the process is nonergodic (Kauffman and Roli 2021a, 2021b).

Imitation without recombination could not generate novelty. But recombination without imitation could not endure. Thus, there is no sense in which the two principles are somehow rivals in an explanation of technology. If the two principles can be separated, then they are related by a simple formula: imitation explains the *survival* of the fittest; combination explains the *arrival* of the fittest. But the use of the term "imitation" in Boyd, Richerson, and Henrich (2013), Henrich (2016), and Muthukrishna and Henrich (2016) is broad enough to include the possibility of recombination. We do not know whether this relatively broad meaning of "imitation" is better than any narrower meaning that might exclude recombination. As far as we can tell, our argument does not depend on sorting out that potentially intricate terminological issue. Whether "imitation" should have a broad or narrow meaning in discussions of cultural evolution, this Element emphasizes the arrival of the fittest and thus makes more reference to combination than imitation.

The positive role of imitation, chance, and error in the evolution of technology is in generating new combinations.

Combination

Adam Smith (1776, I.i.9) explained "improvements in machinery" as resulting in part from "combining together the powers of the most distant and dissimilar objects." Schumpeter (1911 [1934], p. 14) said, "To produce means to combine the things and forces within our reach." Ogburn's 1922 book *Social Change with Respect to Culture and Original Nature* develops the idea of technological evolution by combinations of existing tools or goods. Kauffman (1988, 2008, 2016, 2019) discusses cumulative technological evolution through combinations in the more inclusive framework of the evolution of economic webs of new complements and substitutes. Using patent data and Kaufman's (1993) N-K model, Fleming and Sorenson (2001) test a theory of "invention as a process of recombinant search over technology landscapes." Arthur and Polak (2006) and Arthur (2007, 2009) view cumulative technological change as the production of new goods by combining and recombining old goods. Valverde (2016) also cites Arthur (2009) and says, "recombination of existing structures has been a powerful source of diversity, which is a precondition for cultural evolution." Harper (2018) discusses "new combinations" and innovation in economics. Arthur's theory of combinatorial evolution draws on the gradually emerging field of cumulative technological evolution. Arthur's contribution develops a comprehensive view of technological evolution via combinations and niche creation in the buildout of the economy. Fink et al. (2017) and Fink and Reeves (2019), who cite Arthur (2009), have also represented technological change as recombination. Their model has distinct similarities to ours but, appropriately to their somewhat different scholarly purpose, they assume that the number of useful combinations is fixed ex ante. Our interest in the emergence of novelty requires a more open-ended model.

Weitzman (1998) takes a combinatorial approach to technological change. His model is close to ours. It is mathematically distinct, however, and ours may have the advantage of greater simplicity. Our model also generates the tri-data result we previewed earlier, whereas his model does not. And he preserves the idea that knowledge is a product of planned R&D. More importantly, perhaps, he assumes that there must be a maximum rate of knowledge growth. This assumption led him in a different direction than we have taken. In particular, he focused on the asymptotic growth rate, which is the topic of his "main result," whereas our model exhibits no such slowdown.

In the literature on technological distance, which begins with Griliches (1979), combination and recombination drive technological change. In this literature, the question is often whether combinations of "distant and dissimilar objects" tend to be more valuable than combinations of proximate and similar objects. Nooteboom et al. (2007) and Gilsing et al. (2008) note that as technological distance grows, the knowledge becomes harder to assimilate and apply. This increasing difficulty of "absorption" (Cohen and Levinthal 1990) increasingly offsets the potential novelty benefits of distance and dissimilarity. This trade-off produces an optimal technological distance. "The general influence and importance of optimal technological distance ... has been empirically demonstrated by a number of studies" (Enkel et al. 2018, p. 1260).

The theory of combinatorial evolution has certain advantages over currently available rivals as an explanation of technology. It applies at least from the first appearance of composite tools about 500,000 years ago and it probably applies to the entire history of technology from the earliest known knapped tools of 3.3 million years ago. A theory with such broad evolutionary scope will explain knapped stone tools, the steam engine, and nanotechnology on the same general principles. Such explanatory unity implies explaining the Industrial Revolution without introducing new causes or ad hoc elements. The theory of the combinatorial evolution of technology is best able to reflect in some meaningful way the coevolution of technology, the human body and mind, and human cultures and institutions. It comports well with our knowledge of all these things, including our evolved human psychology. Importantly, the theory of combinatorial evolution is uniquely capable of providing an explanation of the endogenous emergence of novelty in the evolution of the technosphere. And, finally, it is better than its rivals at accounting for the increasing number and complexity of goods over time.

3 The Theory of Combinatorial Evolution

Our theory draws heavily on Arthur (2009). Important elements of the theory can be found in an early essay by Kauffman (1988), who notes "with pleasure the fact that many of the ideas presented here have been discussed by Dr. Brian Arthur, and that Arthur has been thinking about the evolution of such webs with care for some time" (p. 127).

Arthur's "three fundamental principles" are (1) that "technologies, all technologies, are combinations," (2) that "each component of a technology is itself in miniature a technology," and (3) that "all technologies harness and exploit some effect or phenomenon, usually several."

We will modify Arthur's first principle to allow for modifications to an existing good. (Recall that Muthukrishna and Henrich 2016 say, "the three main sources of innovation are serendipity, recombination and incremental improvement.") Boyd, Richerson, and Henrich (2013) give the example of the gradual transformation of the seventeenth-century trade axe into the eighteenth-century felling axe. (Figure 1 illustrates this change.) The latter emerged from the former without new combinations of goods. Presumably, Arthur would say that there is no new "technology" emerging here, which seems correct. Our model, however, counts the number of goods, not technologies. For us, therefore, it is convenient to say that all goods are *either* combinations of other goods *or* modifications of earlier goods.

Arthur's second principle should not be taken to deny that there are the simplest elements of any good from which it is built up, at least if we restrict our attention to physical things. Consider an early spear. Its simplest elements

(a)   (b)

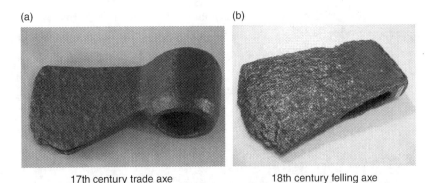

17th century trade axe   18th century felling axe

Figure 1 The 17th century trade axe (a) and the 18th century felling axe (b).

are the stone "point," the adhesive used to "haft" the point to the shaft, and the shaft.[5] And if we consider the actions required to produce each of those techno-units, we come to the elementary actions performed to create them. In the case of the stone point, for example, we come to the knapping actions that caused the point to flake off from the larger stone core. Each of those strikes is a simple element that cannot be broken down into smaller units. But the situation is more ambiguous when we turn to a modern automobile. If we consider only the physical parts, we can descend to the simplest elements, indivisible techno-units such as a bolt or an O-ring. But if we consider the actions required to produce these simplest elements, we are enmeshed in the full autocatalytic web of production (Kauffman 1988, 2008, 2016, 2019; Cazzolli Gatti et al. 2020). We would have to include the actions required to produce the steel-toed boots of the workers who made the bolt, the actions required to produce breakfast for the bootmaker, the actions required to make the plow of the farmer whose corn went into the boot-maker's breakfast, and so on. The simplest elements, in this accounting, sink into ancient time. The factory's involvement in automaking is minute in comparison to the many dispersed actions that make the factory possible. Although the automobile factory may run on the highest Weberian principle of capitalistic rationality, automobiles are not the product of foresight and rational planning. They emerge from the division of labor like stones heaved out of the New England soil by an autumnal frost.

Arthur's third principle explains why recombination produces novelty. For Arthur, an "effect" or "phenomenon" is a kind of "truism of nature that can be exploited and used to a purpose" (p. 46). The "lowly hammer" for example, "depends on the phenomenon of transmission of momentum" and oil refining depends (inter alia) on the phenomenon that different "components or fractions of vaporized crude oil condense at different temperatures" (p. 46). New combinations may take advantage of previously unexploited effects or phenomena, thereby introducing significant novelty to the system. While recombination

---

[5] We simplify by ignoring the question whether the adhesive was itself a combination of two or more ingredients. Zipkin et al. (2014) experiment with glues to which have been added "loading agents" such as quartz or ochre. But Singles and Schoville (2018) report good results using pure *Watsonia* and *Vachellia* glues without loading agents or other ingredients. Presumably, the very earliest adhesives were not compounds but simple glues, which were later displaced by compounds. Jayne Wilkins' team discovered the earliest known stone points, which are about 500,000 years old. In personal correspondence, she has informed us that "we do not know how" these points were hafting to their shafts. It may have been by adhesive. "We cannot say whether they were compound adhesives or not. Another possibility would be strips of animal sinew or other kinds of strings." She expressed pessimism whether residue analysis to ascertain the method of hafting could be successful on the samples available to her "due to their age and their burial history."

without new effects can also produce novelty, the exploitation of effects increases the potential for combinations to produce novelty.

Arthur uses the term "principle" to capture the idea that we know what an effect or phenomenon is and may therefore use it. "A principle . . . is the *idea of use of a phenomenon for some purpose*" (p. 49). We know the engine block has rigid corners that can be used to crack open coconuts. We do not know how much reason and foresight Arthur meant to suggest with that definition of "principle." But his chosen definition suggests a level of understanding that is not necessarily present when old goods are combined to produce new goods. The stone hammers of *Australopithecus afarensis* (McPherron et al. 2010) or of modern Chimpanzees both depend "on the phenomenon of transmission of momentum" even though it may be inappropriate to say that either creature or, indeed, most modern humans have any "*idea* of use of [the] phenomenon."

Arthur's third principle (that an "effect" or "phenomenon" is a kind of "truism of nature that can be exploited and used to a purpose") deserves emphasis because it explains both novelty in general and the great avalanches of novelty seen in the Industrial Revolution and the earlier "efflorescences" discussed by Goldstone (2002). Without an adequate explanation of novelty, any theory of social, cultural, or technological evolution is incomplete and unsatisfactory. Recombination generates novelty, and plenty of it.[6]

Arthur's "effect," "phenomenon," or "truism of nature" is fundamental. Combinations can combine physical objects. We raise an often unrecognized feature of the world: any physical object has some diversity of causal features – truisms of nature – that can be "put to use for a purpose," in a variety of ways alone or with other objects. Think of an engine block. It may be a block of steel 20 inches long, 15 inches deep, and 10 inches wide. The engine block can be used to drill holes, create cylinders, thence an engine. The engine block is rigid and so can be used, and is used, as the chassis of tractors. The engine block is heavy and can therefore be used, a bit excessively, as a paper weight. The engine block is steel. A side of it can be polished to make a mirror. The engine block has sharp rigid corners that can be used to crack open coconuts.

The great diversity of potential causal consequences of any physical object has an important implication. There is *no deductive relation* between these

---

[6] Our argument in this work does not depend on whether we construe the novelty created by recombination as "epistemic" or "ontological." It may be that such novelty is new only for us here inside the system, but predictable for an observer existing beyond the world and somehow looking down on it. (See Devereaux et al. 2021. See also Wolpert 2008, 2017.) Or it may be that that in some deep ontological sense the very possibility of a given combination did not exist before it entered the adjacent possible. In either event, we cannot list all possible future combinations; and in this sense the system's continually arriving novelty is perfectly "real."

different uses.[7] We cannot deduce from the use of an engine block as a chassis that it can be used to crack open coconuts. Evolution is thus propelled by something more tentative, experimental, and arbitrary than deduction. It is propelled by tinkering. The tinkery process of innovation by discovery of new uses is not a deduction. It is a discovery. Our prehuman ancestors made such tinkery discoveries, and we do also.

The great diversity of potential causal consequences of any physical object has another important implication. Diverse causal features of any one object can be combined with diverse causal features of other objects to achieve entirely new effects. A parachute attached to the rear of a small airplane, deployed on landing, becomes an airbrake. The same parachute packed into a chimney causes a mess. Thus, the diversity of "effects" that can be achieved explodes as the number of objects to be combined increases. Here, too, the process is propelled by tinkering. The tinkery process of innovation by combination is not a deduction. It is a discovery. And here as well, our ancestors made such tinkery discoveries in the distant past just as we do today.

Combinatorial evolution uses the materials available to it. In any new combination, the elements being combined already existed for independent reasons. They were not designed with the new combination in mind. The combinations that might be tried at a given moment have, therefore, a tinkery quality. They are cobbled together and may easily be awkward and unlovely. Figure 2 illustrates. The image (first shown to us by Brian Arthur) shows the DeWitt-Clinton locomotive in action along the Mohawk and Hudson line in 1831. (See unattributed 1920, 1921.) The Mohawk and Hudson railroad combined rails and a locomotive, familiar from coal mining, with carriages familiar from horse-drawn passenger transport, thereby creating an early passenger railroad, which ran between Albany and Schenectady. It cobbled together existing elements with some tweaks along the way, such as modifying the wheels on the carriages. The result was clunky and inelegant, at least when compared to later developments.

4 Our Model

Our model of technological change builds on the tinkery theory we have sketched. Nelson and Nelson (2002, p. 731) say, "technology advances through processes that involve both trial and feedback learning, and conscious thought and calculation." Our model reflects this mix of insight and serendipity.

---

[7] Kauffman and Roli (2021a, 2021b) make the ontological claim that the evolution of the biosphere is open ended. The model theoretic proof of Devereaux et al. (2021) supports the epistemic claim that all systems are open-ended for the creatures existing within them even if a view from beyond the system may reveal it to be closed-ended and, in some sense, "deterministic." All three papers support the view that there is no deductive relation between the different uses of a physical object, at least for any creature that might interact with the object.

Figure 2 The image shows the DeWitt Clinton locomotive pulling coaches on the Mohawk & Hudson Railroad. The image was published in the Scientific American in 1920 (Unattributed 1920).

On the side of insight, we have a set of parameters, α_i $(i = 1, 2, 3, ...)$, reflecting the portion of i-tuples of existing goods that are plausible candidates for combination or, in the case of $i = 1$, modification to produce a new good. Only some combinations are plausible candidates to tinker with. Presumably, such plausibility reflects a variety of factors such as the costs of bringing distant goods to a common location. Importantly, however, plausibility is partly a function of human foresight and intelligence. The Wright brothers knew what to combine. They did not try to combine locomotives, ink pots, and mustard seeds.

On the side of serendipity, we assume a fixed probability, P, that a "plausible" combination will generate a new value-enhancing good in the current period. As the number of goods in the system grows over time, the number of "plausible" combinations on which this probability operates will also grow.

We assume the probability value, P, and the plausibility values, α_i, are fixed over time. And we assume our model applies globally without considering differences in technology in different parts of the world or the degree of economic integration across the globe. With these Spartan simplifying assumptions, we apply our model to global data from the last 2,000 years. It is a strength of the model that we get a good fit even with such Spartan assumptions.

We do not imagine that all possible combinations are being surveyed in each period. We make no assumption about what portion of good combinations is actually discovered in any period. A combination is "plausible" only if someone perceives it as such. Perfectly good combinations may go unimagined and untried.

Wadley (2021) says, "By 100,000 years (100 ka) ago, evidence for innovative material culture multiplies, and the modes of innovation become progressively diverse thereafter." Henrich (2016, p. 295) reports that many "bits" of human "know-how and technologies seem to drop in and out of the record and don't make an enduring appearance until the last 100,000 years."[8] If so, the parameters governing recombination (P and the α_i values) could not have stabilized until about 100,000 years ago. In that case, our model, as opposed to our general theory, could not be applied to earlier periods without modification.[9]

Let M_t denote the number of distinct types of goods in the economy at time t. M_t is the degree of cambiodiversity. Our assumption of fixed parameters governing combinations leads to the simple combinatorial model given in equation (1).

$$M_t = M_{t-1} + P\left(\sum_{i=1}^{M_t-1} \alpha_i \binom{M_{t-1}}{i}\right) \qquad (1)$$

where $\binom{M_{t-1}}{i} = \dfrac{M_{t-1}!}{i!(M_{t-1}-i)!}, 0 < P < 1, 0 < \alpha_i < 1$ for $i = 1, 2, \ldots, M_{t-1}$, and $\alpha_{i+1} \leq \alpha_i$ for $i = 1, 2, \ldots, M_{t-1} - 1$. (In practice, we set $\alpha_i = 0$ for $i > 4$.) α_i is the portion of i-tuples of existing goods that are plausible candidates for combination. Therefore, $\alpha_i \binom{M_{t-1}}{i}$ is the pool of candidate i-tuples people might plausibly tinker with, and $P\alpha_i \binom{M_{t-1}}{i}$ is the expected value of the number of new goods created this period by combining i preexisting goods.

---

[8] Scholars are not agreed on what explains the improved continuity and diversity of culture and technology that kicked in about 100,000 years ago. Wadley (2021, pp. 120–121) thinks it was "amplified use of imagination" brought on by anatomical changes reflected in "changes in cranial shape." Henrich says that the sputtering start to cumulative cultural change "is just what you'd expect in a species dependent on a collective brain that was subject to shifting environments, intergroup competition, and challenging ecologies that constrained group size and fractured social ties between bands." Writing at an earlier time, McBreatry and Brooks (2000) reject the idea of a "human revolution" happening 40,000 years ago. They trace "modern behavior" to an earlier species, *H. helmei*, whose behavior was "quite similar to that of modern people." They think the "major adaptive shift" likely happened about 250–300 ka. In the years since McBrearty and Brooks (2000) challenged the "human revolution," evidence has grown for modern behaviors in the ever more distant past (Wilkins et al. 2012, Watts, Chazan, and Wilkins 2016, Blegen 2017, Blegen et al. 2018, Brooks et al. 2018, Potts et al. 2018, Deino et al. 2018, Potts et al. 2020). For example, long-distance exchange (as we note in the text) seems to have emerged over 300,000 years ago. Our model helps to explain how sudden cultural explosions could happen without corresponding anatomical changes. As far as we can tell, however, our argument does not depend on whether the increase in continuity and diversity of culture kicking in about 100,000 years ago corresponded to an important anatomical change in *H. sapiens*.

[9] To capture the dropping out Henrich notes, we would have to add a death term, as Steel, Hordijk, and Kauffman (2020) do.

For simplicity, we take equation (1) to describe the net increase in cambiodiversity ($M_t - M_{t-1}$) rather than separately modeling additions and subtractions to the variety of goods under production. Steel, Hordijk, and Kauffman (2020) include a death term in the equation.

Equation (1) may be called the "TAP equation," where "TAP" stands for "theory of the adjacent possible."[10] The theory was introduced by Kauffman (2000, pp. 142–144), who developed in stark logic the humble insight that evolution happens one step at a time. Amoebae do not give birth to elephants. The way must be prepared. The modern elephant could exist only after evolution had produced mammals and, indeed, the order Proboscidea. At each step some things are possible, others are not. The things possible at any moment are one step away. The *possible* things are *adjacent*. The TAP equation reflects this logic of adjacency because the combinatorial possibilities of the equation grow over time. At earlier moments the number of possible combinations is smaller. *At later moments, the number is larger.*

If technological evolution proceeds one combinatorial step at a time, the *complexity of goods will grow over time*. Reinterpret M_t in the TAP equation as the complexity of the most complex good in the system, where "complexity" means number of component pieces. On this reading, the TAP equation explains the growing differentiation into simple and more complex goods. We conjecture that the TAP equation fits the rate of increase in the complexity of goods over time. If we consider only the number of pieces, the earliest knapped tools were simple. Each had one piece. The earliest compositive tools had three pieces. A modern jet engine has thousands of components. We cannot make a space station without rockets first, and space stations are more complex. So, too, the evolution from carriages to the modern automobile.

We note therefore that the same simple theory, the TAP process, explains simultaneously a glacial then explosive growth in both the number of goods and their increasing differentiation into simple and more complex goods. We know of no other simple model that explains both features at once. Comin and Hobijin (2010), Hughes-Hallett et al. (2014), and Muthukrishna and Henrich (2016) do not derive a hockey stick from a fundamental model. But they agree that the rate of innovation "appears to have been increasing in recent times, as one would expect if innovation is being driven by recombination" (Muthukrishna and Henrich 2016).

We know that the long, slow accumulation of new goods began before the emergence of genus *Homo*, but we don't know how much before. As we have seen, austaloppiths made knapped stone tools at least 3.3 million years ago. They seem to have manufactured only one sort of stone tool, flakes with sharp edges

---

[10] An early version of the TAP equation was formulated in a conversation between Jim Herriot and Stuart Kauffman in August 2017 on Crane Island, Washington. Herriot did the crucial early simulations that revealed the equation's hockey stick behavior and suggested a power law descent distribution.

meant for cutting. Naturally occurring cobbles would be collected and used for two main purposes. They were used as cores to be flaked into smaller bits for use as sharp knives. These cores would be set on an anvil and struck with a percussor to produce flakes with sharp edges (Harmand et al. 2015). Cobbles were also used as anvils or percussors for flaking activities. The flakes seem to have been used to remove flesh from animal bones, which were also smashed with large cobbles or cores, likely to get at the marrow (McPherron et al. 2010). Cobbles or cores were also used to pound food plants.

To produce a flake, Australopithecine manufacturers combined the use of three tools simultaneously: the core, the anvil, and the percussor. Thus, the earliest stone technology we know of in the human evolutionary line entailed "conjunctions of at least three techno-units" (Ambrose 2001, p. 1751), core, anvil, and percussor, to produce a fourth techno-unit, the flake. This combinatorial quality of the technology strengthens our conjecture that the combinatorial evolution of technology began at least 3.3 million years ago with the first knapped stone tools of *Australopithecus afarensis* rather than "only" 500,000 years ago with the composite tools of *Homo heidelbergensis*.

If we were to count the number of stone tools available to the first stone knappers, we might stop at one, judging that only flakes "count" because only flakes were manufactured. But collected cobbles had at least five separate uses as cores, anvils, percussors, bone smashers, and plant pounders. Thus, perhaps we should say that they "really" had six stone tools. Presumably, cobbles were collected before anyone decided which of the five known functions they would be used for. Perhaps we should say, then, that it constituted a separate seventh tool while in that indeterminate state.

Our attempt to count the number of stone tools available to these early toolmakers has run into seemingly insuperable conceptual difficulties. It may be understandable, then, that the scholarly literature contains no successful attempt to count the number of tools or goods available to our various ancestors over time. But perhaps we will be allowed to say that australopithecine knappers had only a "few" stone tools. As far as we know, it cannot be excluded that they also had tools made of decomposable materials such as wood. Presumably, the number of such tools, if they existed, was also "small."

We can probably say that humans had "more" tools by about 200,000 years ago.[11] Shea (2003, pp. 329–330) distinguishes nine separate tools for the

---

[11] There is, of course, nothing magical about 200,000 years ago. It is convenient for our tool-counting exercise, however. The "Levallois" technology, which supplanted the prior Acheulian technology beginning roughly 500,000 years ago, was widespread by 200,000 years ago (Tryon, McBrearty, Texier 2005). And it is widely recognized that it exhibited both local variation and a multiplicity of tools by that time (Shimelmitz and Kuhn 2018).

"Levantine Mousterian" industry of the Middle Paleolithic. Shimelmitz and Kuhn (2018) take a more expansive view of what counts as a separate tool. They note that flakes earlier scholars might have dismissed as "waste" were worked and retouched, suggesting that they were deemed useful by their makers (p. 4).

Shimelmitz and Kuhn (2018) invoke the conceptual difficulties of counting tools when they note the ambiguity in "the boundary between products and byproducts" (p. 2). In spite of the difficulties of counting, the empirical record supports the view that cambiodiversity grew slowly over time before shooting up dramatically with the Industrial Revolution. This view is supported by Beinhocker's (2006, pp. 9, 456–457) estimates that the Yanomami have about 300 distinct goods, whereas there may be about 10 billion distinct goods for sale in New York City.

The TAP process endogenously grows its own expanding economic web (Cazzolla Gatti et al. 2020). Each new good invites new "completing goods" that can be used with it for some purposes, and new "competing goods" for each such purpose. Our vision of ramifying economic development may be similar to that of Jane Jacobs. In *The Nature of Economies*, she wrote, "development without co-development webs is as impossible for an economy as it is for biological development" (Jacobs 2000). The growing web endogenously creates the new niches for yet new goods.

Even more important, this gradual then explosive flowering of the economic web is not "prestatable." Uses of things depend upon the purposes of the user. They are not objective facts of nature. There is no "God's-eye view." Because we cannot deduce the new innovative uses of things with things for known and new unknown purposes, the becoming of the economy cannot be said ahead of time. This is not a failure to predict, as in our incapacity to predict the outcome of a set of fair coin tosses. Certainly, we do not know what will happen. Nor do we know all the outcomes that *can* happen in the evolution of the technosphere. The TAP *equation* bypasses the question of what goods evolve and merely counts the number of them. From this syntactic perspective, we know what can happen. There will be a whole number of goods. But in the TAP *process*, which the TAP equation *reflects*, the semantic question of what gets made (what gets to exist) cannot, in general, be answered ahead of time. It is unprestatable. (See Roli and Kauffman 2020 on semantic vs. syntactic information in the context of open-ended evolution.) Scientific models in the natural and social sciences often – generally we think – assume that the sample space of the process "is known" somehow, though it is not always clear who is imagined to know what. For the TAP process, we do not know the sample space. Therefore, we can have no probability measure.

This unprestatable process is at variance with the powerful mid-century models of Competitive General Equilbrium such as Debreu (1959). Here all possible

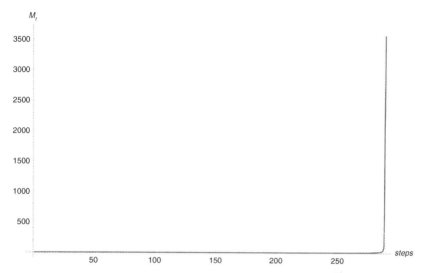

Figure 3 M_t (*y*-axis), scaled from 0 to 2015 (*x*-axis).

dated contingent goods are prestated, and a fixed-point theorem assures at least one price vector for equilibrium. A satisfactory account of what Arthur calls "the build-out of the economy" needs tools of a rather different sort, including tools from modern complexity theory. The TAP process may be of use.

Our equation of the TAP process appears to be new and unique, (Steel, Hordijk, and Kauffman 2020). The TAP process increases glacially for a long time, then explodes upward in the hockey-stick pattern we see in Figure 3 and Figure 4. Cortês et al. (2022) show that with each addition of an item in a TAP process, "it must then take no more than half as many steps to add the next, then half again for another, and so on." Change speeds up over time. Steel, Hordijk, and Kauffman (2020) show that the continuous-time version of the TAP process reaches infinity in finite time with probability one. The intuition is that over time more and more goods are produced within a given time slice such as a year or a day. At some point the rate of change becomes so great that the number of goods produced within a small time slice exceeds any finite number one might name.

The TAP process is superexponential, and it has a singularity. We cannot somehow hit infinity in the real world. What would that mean? Thus, the singularity would be a regime change. It would mark the point at which our model no longer applies. We do not know whether a technological singularity, should it be coming, would be heaven, hell, or something else altogether.

There is a random element in the emergence of new goods, as reflected in the parameter *P*. But only *value-enhancing* goods will have an enduring place in the

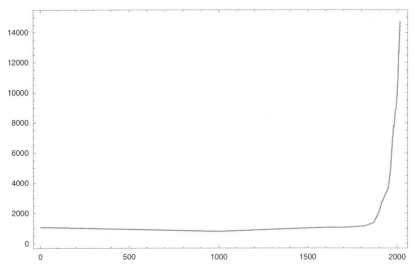

Figure 4 The vertical axis shows GDP per capita in 1990 dollars. The horizontal axis shows the year C. E. Calculated using data from Maddison Project, the Census Bureau, and Kremer (1993).

econosphere, and it is only these value-enhancing goods that we are considering in Equation (1).

The fact that only value-enhancing goods will be produced may not be immediately obvious. But if the purpose of production is consumption, then people will not generally have an incentive to engage in consumption-reducing activities. They will not produce a new and innovative good unless it displaces one or more goods of lower value. Production of the new good will consume resources such as human labor that would otherwise have gone into producing other things including, perhaps, leisure. Thus, whenever a value-enhancing good is added to the system, the overall economic output, GDP, goes up. While errors can and will happen, of course, the tendency is always to produce only such innovative new goods as can cover their opportunity costs with at least some surplus.

Our simple model exhibits the hockey-stick pattern characteristic of economic growth. See Figure 4. Prior to the Industrial Revolution, global GDP per capita fluctuated between about 450 and 700 1990 Geary-Khamis dollars. Already by 1870 (CE) this number had risen to about 870, and thus above historical levels. Global GDP per capita in 2008 was over $7,600, which is about 11 to 17 times larger than historical values. In other words, global per capita GDP today is at least an order of magnitude larger than historical levels. In the richer countries, GDP per capita in 2008 varied between about 20,000 and 30,000 1990 Geary-Khamis dollars (Maddison Project n.d.). Some evidence suggests that our Pleistocene ancestors may have had a standard of life not inferior to historical levels prior to the Industrial Revolution (Clark 2007). If so, the Industrial Revolution had a far greater effect on incomes than did the advent of agriculture and civilization. Some scholars have found evidence that localized regions such as Northern Italy may have reach relatively high incomes well before the Industrial Revolution (Malanima 2011, Van Zanden and van Leeuwen 2012, Alvarez-Nogal and Prados de la Escosura 2013, Broadberry et al. 2015, Dutta et al. 2018). Even if all of these recent results were right, however, they would imply little or no change in the basic global picture of extended stagnation followed by sudden takeoff around 1800.

In the TAP cumulative combinatorial process, a glacially long period of largely unchanging values is followed by a sudden takeoff. This takeoff was the Industrial Revolution. Our model shows that the hockey-stick behavior of human wealth, including the great takeoff of about 1800, emerged from a very simple and unchanging stochastic process. It is not necessary to explain takeoff as the product of some special cause or combination of causes. A low but unchanging value of P will create a long period of stagnation, but sudden takeoff will eventually occur with probability one (Steel, Hordijk, and Kauffman 2020). Thus, the eventual arrival of an industrial revolution was an active possibility once the process of cumulative technological change began with the advent of composite tools some 500,000 years ago or, perhaps, knapped tools some 3.3 million years ago. And it was inevitable once the probability value, P, and the plausibility values, a_i, stabilized 100,000 years ago.[12]

Other explanations of the Industrial Revolution include, inter alia, exploitation of the worker by the capitalist (Marx 1867), Calvinism stimulating the emergence of a unique capitalistic form of economic rationality (Weber 1920, 1927), the emergence of trade-friendly institutions initially brought on by England's Glorious Revolution of 1688 (Dam 2005),[13] the predominance of Christianity in Western culture (Stark 2005), a unique European psychology induced, in part, by the Church's prohibition of cousin marriage (Henrich 2020), genetically determined increases in parental investment in children (Golan and Moav 2002), the supposed beneficial eugenic consequences of English primogeniture (Clark 2007), and a shift in the perceived dignity of commercial activity (McCloskey 2010). Each of these explanations appeals to a special cause (or combination of causes) of the Industrial Revolution, and none has

---

[12] Recall that we are operating with the Spartan assumption that the probability value, P, and the plausibility values, a_i, are fixed over time. We are not saying that a constant, P, and a_i's are a necessary condition of takeoff. Even very low levels for P and the a_i's (whether constant or variable) will eventually generate takeoff if product death rates are below product birth rates.

[13] North and Weingast (1989) is the usual cite for this claim. They were, however, too circumspect for such an unqualified attribution.

emerged as the predominant or consensus view. McCloskey (2006, 2010, 2016) and Koyama and Rubin (2022) are helpful reviews of competing explanations of the Industrial Revolution.

Our radically different explanation of the Industrial Revolution is a deflationary explanation. It *deflates* views that depend on some special cause or combination of causes to account for the sudden takeoff of the Industrial Revolution. Takeoff might have occurred in another time or place. In our model, median income is largely unchanging for a potentially long period before a sudden technological takeoff produces increasingly rapid economic growth. There was no cause of this takeoff that was not present at least 100,000 years earlier when the TAP parameters stabilized. The "cause" of takeoff was the combinatorial explosion whose eventual arrival was essentially certain for at least 100,000 years. It was not the Protestant Ethic, the Glorious Revolution, British primogeniture, or bourgeois dignity that caused the Industrial Revolution. It was slow, grinding probability taking its own sweet time before finally delivering the inevitable combinatorial explosion.

Our theory deflates rivals that rely on some special cause or special combination of causes of the Industrial Revolution. In our model, technological change is driven by the same data-generating process from the earliest days to the present day. There are other explanations that are at least somewhat deflationary, including some of the contributions to modern growth theory (Galor and Weil 2000, Arifovic, Bullard, and Duffy 1997). These models, however, neglect the central fact of cambiodiversity. Nor do they offer a satisfying mechanism for technological change. Some have no mechanism. Finally, apart from the highly parameterized model of Jones (2001), modern growth theory has not clearly demonstrated that it generates hockey stick growth

A deflationist position such as ours is necessarily unable to say why the Industrial Revolution happened just when and where it did. Presumably, some combination of the explanations we deflate helps to explain this when and where. McCloskey (2016, pp. 107–108) seems to hint that "Mongol high-flying" might have produced takeoff had it not been "thrown off course by the Black Death."[14] It is not our view that such explanations must be cast out and trampled underfoot. We claim only that they should be seen as explaining in some degree the timing and location of takeoff. We share the spirit of Crafts (1977), who views "technological progress" as a "stochastic process." He says,

---

[14] Such a hint, however, seems inconsistent with her own view of the supposed historical uniqueness of northwest Europe in recognizing bourgeois dignity.

"the question, 'Why was England first?' is misconceived: the observed result need not imply the superiority of antecedent conditions in England" (p. 434). Similarly, in our view, the timing of takeoff owes much to chance.

Our model suggests that the wealth explosion of the Industrial Revolution may have been a combinatorial explosion in the unchanging process of technological change as modeled by the TAP equation. Our model allows us to explain the Industrial Revolution without introducing new causes or ad hoc elements. This absence of special precipitating causes is a strength our explanation shares with the models of unified growth theory. The simple growth-theory model given in the next section suggests how our model of technological change could be profitably integrated with this theory.

5 Our Tri-Data Result

Modern Growth Theory *(by Abigail Devereaux)*

Our combinatoric model can contribute to modern growth theory by offering a more satisfactory model of technological change. In unified growth theory, the system moves endogenously from a "Malthusian" regime of low growth and steady income, to a "Post-Malthusian" regime of higher growth and increasing incomes, to, finally, a "Modern Growth regime" of continued technological advance in which, however, population growth no longer increases with income, but instead declines (Galor and Weil 2000, Dutta et al. 2018). In these models, technological change is measured by a scalar whose rate of growth is influenced by the amount of prior knowledge investment. The fundamental form of this process is typically represented as Equation (2),

$$Y_t = A_t K_t^\beta L_t^{(1-\beta)}, \tag{2}$$

where Y is the output of the economy, and K and L are capital and labor. The symbol "A_t" represents "knowledge." Given constant K and L, an increase in A_t increases total productivity of the economy. The theory is "endogenous" growth theory because A_t can change over time endogenously to the model. (Endogenous growth models can be traced to Romer 1990.) In this sort of model, the driver of change (A_t) may be labeled "education," "R&D," "the number of people engaged in producing ideas" (Jones 2001), or something else. These models generally assume that "all knowledge resides in the head of some individual person and the knowledge of a firm, or economy, or any group of people is simply the knowledge of the individuals that comprise it" (Lucas 2009). In this sort of "idea-based theory of growth" (Jones 2001), resources are diverted from consumption or other productive activities and invested in

knowledge production. The mechanism linking such investments to technological change is vague or unspecified.

The following model is a "unified model" of this type, but with our combinatorial model of technological change deployed to explain technological change.
Our M_t from equation (1) replaces the A_t in equation (2). As far as we know,
Jones (2001) is the only other endogenous growth model that has been shown to
produce the hockey stick of economic growth. We recognize that our model is as
simplistic as it is simple. Our goal is only to illustrate as simply as possible how
our model of technological change can be integrated with existing economic
models of growth to generate a "unified model" that conforms with the leading
facts of economic history.

In our simple discrete time model, Y_t is world GDP in period t. K_t is the
capital stock in period t. It is the value of all goods used to generate, ultimately,
final output. L_t is the stock of labor. We assume that each living person provides
the same quantity of labor, which we normalize to one. Thus, L_t is also the
population in period t. We measure technology by cambiodiversity, M_t. For this
simple model, we assume that output is generated by an aggregate production
function of the Cobb–Douglas type. Thus,

$$Y_t = M_t K_t^{\beta} L_t^{(1-\beta)}, \tag{3}$$

where beta is between 0 and 1.

The capital stock, K_t, is increased by saving, which we assume to be a fixed
fraction, s, of output. It is diminished by use as, for example, when machines
wear out over time. This "depreciation" occurs at the fixed rate delta. Thus,
growth in the capital stock is described by the following equation:

$$K_{t+1} = sY_t + (1 - \delta)K_t, \tag{4}$$

where s and δ are between 0 and 1.

In the standard economic models of modern growth theory, the population
growth rate is derived from the utility-maximizing choices of individuals
deciding how many children to have and how much to invest in each child.
For the sake of simplicity, and to focus on cambiodiversity, we take population
L_t to be exogenous, derived in part from the estimates in (Kremer 1993) and
augmented with numbers from the US Census Bureau.

We calibrate the model to reasonably fit growth in total world output from
1 CE to 2015 CE, adjusted for inflation and measured in 2011 international
dollars (Maddison Project n.d.).

We assume that α_i is a decreasing function as i increases, and that $\alpha_i = 0$
for $i > 4$. In particular, we assume the decreasing function takes the form

$$\alpha_i = \begin{cases} \dfrac{1}{(i\theta)^\rho}, & i \leq 4 \\ 0, & i > 4 \end{cases} \qquad (5)$$

where $\theta > 0, \rho > 0$. The list of parameters is given in Table 1.

Although we require values for eight parameters to simulate the model, we have only four that we can adjust: M_0, P, θ, and ρ. The remaining four are externally given in one way or another. Population levels are data. Following the economics literature, we choose 1/3 for capital's share of output (Kremer 1993, Jones and Romer 2010) and values $s = 0.25$, delta $= 0.06$. We are further constrained by the requirements (noted again shortly) that the model be coherent before 1 CE and that the capital stock does not shrink as output grows.

Figure 5 shows the estimated progression of total world GDP from 1 CE to the present together with simulated values under three different parameterizations. Note that it is simple to extend the simulation backwards from 1 CE by decreasing the initial number of distinct goods M_0. We consider it important that the model has validity before 1 CE. Importantly, the capital stock K_t should not shrink as output Y_t grows. We chose our parameters to ensure the model is coherent prior to 1 CE. The value of P in combination with the parameters θ, ρ (which determine α_i) determine how easy or difficult it is to come up with viable products. A higher P, a lower θ, or a lower ρ, all else equal, is correlated with a larger ΔM_t and therefore a larger ΔY_t.

As we have seen, our model explains the Industrial Revolution. It explains the hockey stick of economic growth. Unfortunately, this good hockey stick has an evil twin, which is the crisis of the Anthropocene. It seems fair to say that most participants in public discourse have given attention to one hockey stick while ignoring or downplaying the other. The hockey stick of economic growth, the good twin, has allowed humanity to swell to over 8 billion persons. And it has allowed most of those human souls to escape the pain, poverty, and premature death characteristic of all earlier ages. If we focus on the good hockey stick and neglect its evil twin, economic growth is a panacea. Damn the torpedoes; full speed ahead! But there is good reason to fear that the crisis of the Anthropocene threatens continued progress in human welfare. Some observers are alarmed enough to suggest "degrowth," conceived as "a radical political and economic reorganization leading to reduced resource and energy use" (Kallis et al. 2018).

Our own views are not uniform on this topic beyond the agreement on the banalities that human welfare is good and climate change is bad. There is a trade-off, however, between human welfare and environmental degradation, at least in the short run. And current knowledge does not allow us to escape that trade-off. Radical degrowth would plunge billions back into poverty and,

Table 1 Baseline parameter values of the combinatorial growth model, defined by Equations (3), (4), and (5). Entries with comma-delimited values demonstrate more than one good candidate parameter.

Parameter	Value(s)	Comments
Y_0	1.82741×10^{11}	Total world GDP at $t = 0$
M_0	$50, 88$	Number of distinct value-adding goods at $t = 0$
P	~ 0.0006	The master probability of a successful combination
θ	6	$P\alpha_i = P \frac{1}{(i\theta)^P}$ is the probability that a combination of i goods results in a new good
ρ	2	$P\alpha_i = P \frac{1}{(i\theta)^P}$ is the probability that a combination of i goods results in a new good
L_0	1.7×10^8	Total world population at $t = 0$
β	$1/3$	Capital's share of output
s	0.25	Fraction of output reinvested into capital formation
δ	$0.06, 0$	Capital depreciation rate

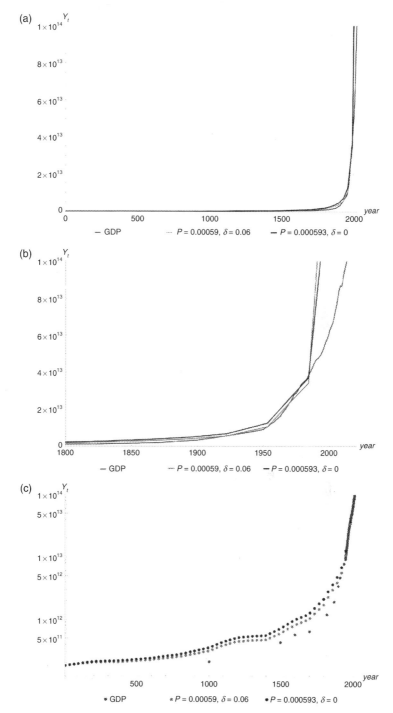

Figure 5 The top graph shows total world GDP (blue) plotted from 1 CE to 2015 CE, together with the parameterization $\{M_0 = 50, \delta = 0.06\}$ (yellow), $\{M_0 = 50, \delta = 0\}$ (green), and $\{M_0 = 88, \delta = 0.06\}$ (red). The middle figure is the same graph, zoomed in to 1800 CE to 2015 CE, to better visually differentiate between the parameterizations. The bottom figure is the same parameterizations plotted on a log GDP scale, from 350 CE to 2015 CE.

indeed, produce widespread death and suffering. But inaction on the looming prospect of a mass extinction event and on climate may not be sustainable for the species. Our zoological theory of technological change is informative on both the nature of the problem and the possibilities for ameliorative change. We hope to return to this topic in future works.

We noted earlier that we have only four free parameters and that we were further constrained by the requirements that that model be coherent before 1 CE and that the capital stock does not shrink as output grows. Given these constraints and the size of our dataset, it would be difficult adjust these four parameters to get a good fit to an arbitrarily chosen model. In other words, our good fit is strong evidence in favor of the TAP model. This already strong evidence is further strengthened by our results on a very different dataset, as we now explain.

Descent Distribution in Patent Data *(by Sergi Valverde)*

Patent data provide another way to test the TAP model of equation (1). Patents are well-defined objects introducing a novel design, method, or solution for a given problem or a set of problems. Thus, they give us a record of innovations, albeit an incomplete one.[15] Existing databases store multiple levels of patent description and they can be analyzed in full detail. Additionally, they indicate what previous novelties have been required to build new ones. This dataset of patents and their citations defines a patent citation network $G = (V, L)$ (Valverde et al., 2007). A node $v_i \in V$ represents an individual patent, and the directed link (v_i, v_j) indicates that patent v_i is a (direct) descendent of patent v_j and, conversely, patent v_j is a predecessor of patent v_i. The citation network is directed and acyclic (see Figure 6). Each patent v_i may have many immediate predecessors, denoted $k(i)$, and many immediate descendants, denoted $d(i)$. In addition, each patent indirectly depends on all its predecessors, parents, grandparents, great grandparents, and so on, right back to the root node. We can define the set of all direct and indirect ancestors *to* any patent, denoting it $K(i)$. And we can define the set of all direct and indirect descendants *from* any patent, denoting it $D(i)$.

As we explain presently, we have found a power-law distribution in the $D(i)$ values. We may speak of a power law when one variable moves as the power of another, at least approximately and for sufficiently large values of the driving variable. In the simplest such relationship,

---

[15] Patent data are incomplete because, roughly, certain innovations and their progeny have been trimmed out. Our results will be meaningful if the metaphorical trimming process has not fundamentally changed over our sample period. We thank Marina Rosser for pressing upon us the difference between patents and innovations.

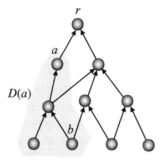

Figure 6 The dataset of patents forms a large, directed acyclic network, where links trace the citation of older, predecessor patents (*r*) in the newer, descendant patents (*b*). The set of descendants of node (a), *D(a)*, is the green shaded area. It includes every node that can be accessed (directly or indirectly) from it by an uninterrupted chain of intermediate inventions.

$$F(x) = y^y. \tag{6}$$

We have a *power-law distribution* for a random variable if

$$\Pr(X \geq x) \sim cx^y. \tag{7}$$

Mitzenmacher (2003, p. 232) says that Pareto (1896) contains the "earliest apparent reference" to a power law. Mitzenmacher's list of other early examples includes Estoup (1916), Zipf (1932), and Lotka (1926). Simon (1955a) is the earliest work we know of to discuss power laws as a large and distinct class of mathematical functions with an indefinite variety of applications.

There is a network-theoretic literature finding power laws in patent data (Bentley et al. 2004, Chen and Hicks 2004, Strandburg et al. 2006, Bedau 2014). In this literature, power laws are found in the number of *immediate* predecessors or descendants, the k and d values as defined earlier, rather than the number of direct and *indirect* predecessors or descendants, the K and D values as defined earlier. Valverde et al. (2007), for example, study US patent data from 1975 to 2005. They find that that the "in-degree distribution" for the patent citation network follows an extended power-law shape. In other words, for k as defined earlier, they find that $P(k) \sim (k + k_0)^{-\gamma}$, as described by the Zipf–Mandelbrot function with an exponent $\gamma \approx 4$. They attribute the size of this empirical exponent of the patent network to "preferential attachment and power-law aging." We have not found prior work examining the possibility of a power law in the $D(i)$ values, the total number of immediate and indirect descendants.

Steel, Hordijk, and Kauffman (2020) have shown that the TAP process of equation (1) generates a power law in the $D(i)$ values. They explain, "each time a new item is produced from a combination of i existing items, then this new item is regarded as a descendant of each of the i items that produced it, as well as

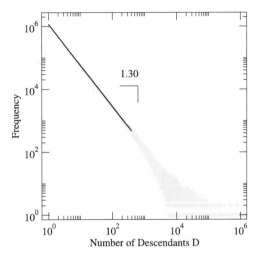

Figure 7 Empirical frequency distribution $P(D)$ of the number D of patent descendants. The solid line depicts the best-fitting scaling $P(D) \sim D^{-1.30}$.

a descendant of all the earlier items that have i as an ancestor. This gives rise to a *descent distribution* which describes the proportion of items having $0, 1, 2, \ldots$ descendants." They measured the power-law coefficients arising from multiple simulations of the TAP process under a range of parameter values. Their simulations yield a range of values for the power-law coefficient ranging from about -1.1 to -1.35. (See their figure 3.) Using US Patent and Trademark Office (USPTO) patents filed between 1835 and 2010, we found a power-law distribution with a coefficient of -1.3. See Figure 7.

Steel, Hordijk, and Kauffman (2020) note, "The exact slope of the power law depends on the model parameters." We nevertheless find it striking that our empirical value falls within the range emerging from their simulations. This proximity of values becomes more striking when we consider how close our fitted growth-theoretic model is to the simulations of Steel, Hordijk, and Kauffman (2020). Like our growth-theoretic model earlier, their simulations used the discrete-time version of the TAP equation with their death term set to zero and have the α_i decreasing as i increases, with $\alpha_i = 0$ for $i > 4$. This close conformity between two components of our tri-data result is extraordinary given that the two procedures test different things and use radically different data.

Complexity of Tools over Time

Data on the number of techno-units per tool provide a third way to test the TAP model of equation (1). Unfortunately, there does not seem to be enough satisfactory numerical data to permit a statistical test of the model's prediction of increasing tool complexity.

Each of the earliest stone tools had just one piece. Toyota claims that a modern automobile has about 30,000 pieces (Toyota n.d.). However accurate Toyota's number might be, it suggests a great increase in the complexity of tools over time. Kline and Boyd (2010) find a linear relationship between the logarithm of mean techno-units per tool and the logarithm of population size for marine foraging technology in ten small-scale societies in Oceania. If this relationship holds for all population levels, the tool complexity will have risen more rapidly after 1800 than before, although not superexponentially as our model predicts. But applying their model to the Industrial Revolution and beyond is probably too great an extrapolation.

Unfortunately, although we have data such as Toyota (n.d.), Perreault et al. (2013), and Kline and Boyd (2010), there does not seem to be enough satisfactory numerical data to permit a statistical test of this prediction. But the data we do have are consistent with our model.

6 Niche Theory

The TAP model of equation (1) implies that the number of goods exchanged multiplies and ramifies over time.[16] It implies, therefore, a similar multiplication and ramification of economic opportunities, which Arthur (2009 pp. 174–176) calls "opportunity niches." In our theory, each new good creates new economic niches and, therefore, new possibilities for more innovative goods. Consider mouse pads. There was no latent market for mouse pads in 1870 or in 1970. Any attempt to sell "mouse pads" would surely have failed. No one had a use for them. There was no latent demand. Once personal computers with graphical interface software began to be sold to ordinary households, however, an economic niche for mouse pads came to be. The arrival of the computer mouse created the possibility of selling mouse pads. It opened a latent market, which became actual and overt once suppliers began to offer them. Once the public had computer mouses, it could instantly understand what a "mouse pad" is and why a person might want one. The economic niche came into existence when the first computer mouse was sold. Presumably, however, it was only some time after the niche opened that an "alert entrepreneur" (Kirzner 1973) first noticed the opportunity and acted on it.

Economic goods and relations, like species in an ecosystem (Cazzolla Gatti 2011), grow increasingly diverse and complex over time. This ramifying complexity is a central feature of economic life, and yet it is largely absent from the dominant models of modern economics. Following Mandeville (1729), Smith (1776), Menger (1871), A. A. Young (1928), Beinhocker (2006), Arthur (2009),

---

[16] This section reproduces large passages of Cazzolla Gatti et al. (2020).

and others, we recognize that economic growth entails an increase in the variety of goods produced, which (as we have seen) Koppl et al. (2015) call "cambio-diversity." But, just as new species need new biological niches, new goods require new economic niches. There must be a latent market, that is, a new economic niche for the good to enter, which arises out of a larger economic system. If there is, then the entering good transforms the latent market into an active market. There must first be the niche, the latent market. Then the good can enter. And if it does, it will produce new niches, one or more of which might be filled by other new goods. Our theory of the evolution of economic niches explains how they emerge and ramify over time as technology evolves.

Our theory generalizes our mouse pad example. It follows from the parallel emergence of ecological niches proposed by Cazzolla Gatti et al. (2018). An economic niche might be called a "latent market." For our purposes here, a market is just an ongoing set of exchanges. These exchanges might be supported by various physical structures, social habits, legal institutions, and so on. As Hodgson (2007, p. 326) notes, "markets involve social norms and customs, instituted exchange relations, and information networks that have to be explained." We endorse the view that the institutional enablers of economic exchange require (evolutionary) explanation. Our current focus on niche emergence in the evolution of the technosphere, however, allows us to leave all such enabling institutions in the background for the time being. We follow Cazzolla Gatti et al. (2020) in applying Haldane's (1956) analysis of time in biology to the role of institutions in the evolution of the technosphere.

In this section, we are focusing on the evolution of the technosphere and how that evolution creates a ramifying process of niche creation. Thus, we ignore the possibility that some desirable good becomes technologically possible but cannot find a market because of "institutional" factors such as weak property rights. Such possibilities are quite real. Weak property rights in medieval China, for example, thwarted innovation (Lowery and Baumol 2013). Our model of niche evolution assumes a favorable institutional environment only as a first approximation that should be dropped when it is convenient to do so.

Thus, again, in this analysis a "market" is just a set of exchanges. An economic niche is a potential or latent market. It is a market that could be created if a potential seller would only offer the relevant product. As we said earlier, each new good creates new economic niches and, therefore, new possibilities for more innovative goods. Some of those possibilities are realized, thereby creating yet more niches for yet more goods. In this way the number and variety of economic niches grow over time.

New goods spawn new economic niches, which lead to more goods and more new niches. Over time, the number and variety of goods and the number and variety of economic niches grow. This is not to deny, however, that unfilled niches may fall away over time. In the past, we may imagine, there was an economic niche for an innovative buggy whip made of birch bark. No one filled the niche, however, and today there is no latent demand for birch-bark buggy whips. Although some niches fall away, increasing cambiodiversity entails increasing numbers and varieties of economic niches.

Just as biological species exist in autocatalytic ecosystems (Cazzolla Gatti et al. 2017), market goods exist in autocatalytic economic systems. If a new good is to be successful, if it is to add value to the system, it must be sold on a market. In other words, it must occupy an economic niche. Our notion of "niche" is similar or identical to Brian Arthur's notion of "opportunity niche," and his examples are illuminating (2009 pp. 174–176). Arthur makes our central point that new niches lead to new goods that lead to further new niches. He speaks of "technologies creating opportunity niches that call forth technologies." He says, "Opportunity niches change as the collective technology changes; and they elaborate and grow in numbers as the collective grows." Arthur provides important theoretical insights without attempting a formal model of niche creation, such as we provide.

A variety of goods may be sold in a given market, as when apple pie and peach cobbler compete for dessert customers. And, a given good may be sold in multiple markets, as when apple pies are sold in both London and Berlin. But the great increases in cambiodiversity that we have seen on all timescales since the arrival of "composite tools" perhaps 300,000 years ago (Ambrose 2001) required the emergence of new economic niches just as the Cambrian diversity explosion of biological species (Conway 2006) necessitated the emergence of new ecological niches. In our earlier example, there must be a niche for mouse pads before mouse pads can succeed in the economy. A theory of increasing cambiodiversity, therefore, requires a theory of the evolution of economic niches that would be similar to that of ecological niches (Cazzolla Gatti et al. 2018) or even, perhaps, formally identical to it.

Our humble example of the mouse pad suggests the core insight we stated earlier: new goods create new economic niches, some of which are filled by further new goods, thus creating further new niches. We attempt to give this insight solid analytical foundations, drawing on models of niche emergence in ecology. Thus, while we address ourselves to the economics profession at large, our model of niche emergence is also a contribution to evolutionary economics (see e.g., Law 1705, Mandeville 1729, Smith 1776, Veblen 1898, A. A. Young 1928, Schumpeter 1911, Hodgson and Knudsen 2010). Our model of niche emergence reveals a sense in which cooperation is an inherent feature of biological and market competition.

Emergent Economic Niches Mitigate Competitive Pressures

Ecological niches are filled by the best-fitted species or guilds of species. They are "best" compared to their rivals, but they will not generally be "optimal" from a design perspective. Natural selection grades on a curve. Although species can initially compete (or, better, find a way to avoid competition with others by ecological niche displacement [Ulanowicz 1997]), usually they evolve toward symbiotic relationships (symbiosis, mutualism, commensalism, etc.), shifting their interactions from competition to cooperation, which allows the emergence of even more potential ecological niches (Ulanowicz 1997, Fath 2007, Cazzolla Gatti et al. 2017, 2018). Similarly, economic niches are filled by best-fitted goods. And they are "best" only when compared to their rivals. They may not be optimal from some absolute point of view. Market competition grades on a curve. These "best" goods coevolve in the "economic web" of all the goods related as competing and completing goods (Matutinović 2002).

As noted earlier, new goods typically come into existence as competing to some currently existing goods and completing to others. Hence, the web evolves into its "adjacent possible" sucked into the very opportunity it itself creates (Kauffman 2019). More, although companies or workers can initially compete, they often find ways of avoiding competition with others by economic niche displacement, which may produce an outcome similar to monopolistic competition. A firm may occupy a unique economic niche because it has differentiated its product. Such differentiations may help a set of potentially rivalrous firms to evolve toward "symbiotic" relationships (cooperatives, holdings, etc.), shifting their interactions from competition to cooperation, which allows the emergence of even more potential economic niches.

Agent heterogeneity is endogenous in our model, which allows us to avoid the sort of paradoxes explored by the economist G. B. Richardson (1960, 2003). He has fun with paradoxes created by the economist's notion of "perfect competition." In a "perfectly competitive" market, you have an infinite number of potential entrants waiting to enter a market. The slightest sliver of "economic profit" induces entry. But, Richardson asks, if we assume (as the theory does) "perfect information," won't all of those infinitely many potential entrants enter? But if they do, won't the resulting massive entry induce massive losses? Anticipating this, won't they abstain from entering? In this perfect competition scenario, the profit opportunity everyone knows about goes unexploited. And so on. Richardson (1960, p. 248) says, "[a] profit opportunity which is available equally for everyone is, in fact, available to no one at all." The logic here is not so different from Brian Arthur's (1994) El Farol problem. El Farol is a small, local bar and common after-work hangout place in Santa Fe, New Mexico. Given the size constraints of the bar if too many people went on the same evening (Thursday, in the original formulation), then the large crowd would diminish each individual's experience. However, and in contrast, if too few people went to the bar that evening, then the experience was also suboptimal for lack of critical participation. The point is there is no equilibrium solution that can be worked out in advance. The situation creates a kind of permanent disequilibrium in part because the best choice (go or don't go) for each individual depends on the unknown choices of all the other individuals. The self-referential nature of the problem calls for approaches quite different from those of standard economics.

An important part of what drives Richardson's paradoxes is the assumption of agent homogeneity. Without the notion of an economic niche, the notion of agent heterogeneity is ad hoc. By introducing the notion of niche, we are able to make agent heterogeneity endogenous. Agents are not "just different" from one another. Rather, they occupy different positions in the system and have, therefore, different opportunities to acquire skills, invest, learn about local market conditions, and so on. We do not deny that some differences among persons are genetic. Such a denial would contradict modern Darwinism. Indeed, a theory of gene–culture coevolution requires the assumption of genetic differences across organisms, without which there could be no anatomical changes in hominin evolution. But the genetic differences among modern humans at a moment in time are mostly inconsequential and do little or no intellectual work in our theory, at least if we can neglect the charged issue of sex.[17] Each person begins life with about the same potential and the same human nature. But their different positions in the social system will shape them differently. This view of human equality resonates deeply with Adam Smith's ideas on human equality, which he expressed forcefully in the second chapter of *The Wealth of Nations*.

A cornerstone concept in ecology also resonates with our Smithian vision of human equality. The Competitive Exclusion Principle states that no two species can occupy the same niche, thus, it is invoked as a driver for species diversification and niche creation. The ensuing heterogeneity stabilizes competitor dynamics, avoiding their competition. Something similar is true in economics: in economic niches, differences reduce interfirm competition and enhance the number of coexisting firms.

In the economy, goods and services afford niches for not-yet-existing competing and completing goods. For example, word processing on personal computers afforded the possibility to share files and created a niche for a new good: the modem. But there was not a complete market for modems before their

---

[17] That there are genetic differences between the sexes is indisputable. It is less clear precisely how those genetic differences matter beyond a few obvious things such as pregnancy and lactation. Much hangs on how one resolves questions of how sex matters, but our argument does not.

invention. Someone saw the new opportunity and seized that opportunity to make and sell modems. This gets to Richardson's paradox. Without the notion of an economic niche, the modem is an opportunity for everyone and thus, perhaps, for no one. But, if we recognize the role of niche emergence and the paucity of parties proximate to a newly opened niche, then we can avoid Richardsonian paradox. Competitive General Equilibrium (CGE) cannot help us work out the dynamics of innovation because it requires us to prestate all dated contingent goods, which is to say that it assumes away novelty. We could not prestate the to-be-invented modem. Thus, again, we need to look in a new direction, namely, toward a theory of economic niche emergence.

Thus, we arrive at a sensible notion of "economic niche." In economics, the word "niche" is used often enough to represent a specialized market at the macroscale, or the activity an individual is best fitted for at the microscale. However, we do not know of any good, clear analysis of what, precisely, an economic niche might be. Here, we attempt to formally define a notion of economic niche adumbrated in Koppl et al. (2015) and show that this notion of "niche" is strongly related to that of "ecological niche" and is a missing piece from the theory of economic growth and development. Noting that niche derives from the Latin, *nidus*, meaning nest, the ecological context takes prior usage. In fact, economic growth models ignore cambiodiversity (as defined earlier). If the economy is an evolutionary system, then cambiodiversity must be central to economic growth, but we cannot have a fully coherent model in which cambiodiversity grows unless a model contains a coherent notion of "niche" and niche "emergence."

A Parallel between the Ecological and Economic Niche

There is a parallel between a niche as a market and a species as a good or service. The economic web grows into its adjacent possible opportunities and thus creates its own growing diversity, which leads to the growing econosphere and the autocatalytic emergence of cambiodiversity.

For an ecosystem to function and to persist over time, several critical roles must be filled and maintained (in the role of completing the task), including energy acquisition (plants/primary producers), energy concentrators/dissipators (animals/consumers), and nutrient releasers (decomposers). Early humans, as hunter-gatherers, differed little from this arrangement.

The arrival of agriculture greatly enhanced energy acquisition leading to both population growth and nonagricultural specializations. This can be considered as a clear example of niche emergence in human societies. But it should not be considered the first example or even a particularly early example. Long-distance trade and, therefore, niche emergence long preceded the emergence of sedentary agriculture.

Brooks et al. (2018) document evidence of hominin trade networks about 300,000 years ago. Their evidence suggests that trade with strangers, or at least beyond the band, emerged between 300,000 years ago and 500,000 years ago. Thus, exchange networks seem to have come either before the emergence of *Homo sapiens* or coincident with it.[18] Their evidence is the apparent use of obsidian from distances up to 50 km, which exceeds the "likely home range . . . of a small family-based band" of 20 km. Tools manufactured on site were made of obsidian gathered from such distances. Potts et al. (2020) note that stone transport distances in the earlier Acheulean technology were "[n]o more than 5 km."[19]

Watts, Chazan, and Wilkins (2016) find that the jaspilite of flakes and blades found in a site in South Africa (Canteen Kopje) was carried to the site from a distance of at least 90 km at least 300,000 years ago. They do not address whether long-distance materials transport is evidence of trade networks. But if Brooks et al. (2018), Blegen (2017), Marwick (2003), and McBrearty and Brooks (2000) are right to make such a link for obsidian, then, presumably, we may view long-distance transport of jaspilite as evidence of trade networks existing at least 300,000 years ago.

Watts, Chazan, and Wilkins (2016) also find evidence that specularite was transported about 170 km to the Wonderwerk cave in South Africa at least 300,000 years ago. This powdery material would have been used as a bodily decoration, perhaps in rituals. Watts, Chazan, and Wilkins (2016) link the emergence of ritual and symbolic culture to the emergence of composite tools about 500,000 years ago.[20]

---

[18] Trade might have emerged coincident with our species if it emerged about 300,000 years ago. This date depends on accepting the judgment of Hublin et al. (2017) that their find should be classified as *H. sapiens*, which is not universally accepted. And, as Bergstrom et al. (2021, p. 231) say, "it is not conceptually meaningful to describe the time depth of the population structure of early modern humans with point estimates."

[19] The Acheulean technology spanned a period from about 1 or 2 million years ago (see note 24) to about 500,000 years ago. Brooks et al. (2018) give us evidence of long-distance transport of materials in the Middle Stone Age, and their earliest example is about 300,000 years ago. Thus, there is a gap in our knowledge of this topic for the period spanning roughly 500,000 years ago to 300,000 years ago.

[20] It is widely but not universally accepted that the early uses of ochre and specularite included its use in rituals or as symbols or signals. The thesis of "female cosmetic coalitions" (FCC) holds that females within the band formed coalitions to induce greater male cooperation in child rearing. Pigments, especially red ochre, were important tools of these female coalitions. While affirming the "importance of pigment" beginning at least 300,000 years ago, McBrearty and Brooks (2000) are cautious about FCC, viewing it as an "idiosyncratic" interpretation of the evidence. The leading alternative theory holds that pigments were used for cheap but honest signals supporting group cohesion. A leading author of this theory treats FCC respectfully but

In spite of her role in establishing long-distance materials displacement for specularite and jaspilite in South Africa at least 300,000 years ago, Wilkins (2020, p. 124) says, "While much has been made of transport distances of 'exotic' raw material in the South African MSA, we actually still have very little conclusive evidence for long-distance exchange." Her doubts include doubts that materials found on site came from far away. She describes the evidence of "long-distance transfers [in South Africa] extending back to before the origins of Homo sapiens" as "speculative" (p. 124). Her discussion (pp. 123–124) of some earlier and now somewhat debunked results on long-distance materials transport is informative.

Blegen (2017) documents obsidian transport distances of up to 166 km occurring about 200,000 years ago. He suggests that such transfers could be a result of exchange, of "very mobile hunter-gatherer group[s]," or of both (pp. 14–15). Blegen et al. (2018) offer the "refined age of 222.5 ± 0.6 ka for early evidence of long-distance (166 km) obsidian transport at the Sibilo School Road Site." The earlier results of Marwick (2003) and McBrearty and Brooks (2000) supported the hypothesis of long-distance trade at least 130,000–140,000 years ago.

The hypothesis that trade networks emerged with or prior to the emergence of modern humans is strengthened by evidence on hominin social structure. Boyd and Richerson (2021) review evidence suggesting "that large-scale cooperation occurred in the Pleistocene societies that encompass most of human evolutionary history." They believe the time depth of such "large-scale cooperation with unrelated individuals" is deep enough that "our psychology evolved in such a world and that mechanisms like other-regarding preferences . . . are adaptations shaped by natural selection because they support large-scale cooperation."

Ancient hominin social structures may have enabled the emergence of exchange networks. Domínguez-Rodrigo et al. (2019) find evidence of "meta-group social networks" in archaic humans. Domínguez-Rodrigo et al. (2019) say, "A substantial part of human social relations occurs outside the living group. In modern foragers, this results in the continuous fluidity of individuals among groups and the relationships of individuals from different groups"

finds it ultimately "poorly supported and unconvincing" Kuhn (2016). Watts, Chazan, and Wilkins 2016 attribute the theory to Kuhn, who claims to be "[f]ollowing the lead" of Maynard-Smith and Harper (2003). It's costly signals in the context of conflicting interests versus cheap signals in the context of harmony. Wadley et al. (2004) emphasize the practical uses of ochre including its value in tanning leather and in hafting stone points to wooden shafts. "Archaeologists can no longer assume that the presence of ochre in a site is automatically and exclusively equated with ritual and symbolic behaviour" (Wadley et al. 2004, p. 672). Their study does not let us know if this or other utilitarian uses of ochre were present from the beginning of composite tool use or arose only later. In any event, nothing in our explanation of technology depends on just how pigments were initially used.

(p. 62). They provide evidence of a similar social structure for *Homo habilis* and *Homo erectus*. (See also the special issue of the *Journal of Human Evolution* introduced by Goren-Inbar and Belfer-Cohen 2020.) The Dunbar numbers for these archaic humans, based on the average sizes of their neocortices (relative to overall brain size), exceed the group sizes inferred from the archeological record. This difference in group-size estimates can be reconciled by positing meta-group social networks.

The famous "Dunbar number" of 150 for humans (Dunbar 1992, Aiello and Dunbar 1993) is really only one of several Dunbar numbers for humans and other hominids. Dunbar (1998, p. 187) said, "the various human groups that can be identified in any society seem to cluster rather tightly around a series of values (5, 12, 35, 150, 500, and 2,000) with virtually no overlap in the variance around these characteristic values." Thus, even for *H. sapiens* there are really several Dunbar numbers. Dunbar (2020) develops the point and modifies the "series of values" given in Dunbar (1998). He now gives a benchmark value of 1,500 for tribe size. Dunbar (2021) is a recent book-length treatment of the issues.

Pearce and Moutsiou (2014 p. 12) find that the late-Pleistocene obsidian transfer distance of about 200 km corresponds to the "geographic ranges" of "the ~1500-strong ethnolinguistic tribe" of "recent hunter–gatherers." It is not clear how to read this result backward in time to the origin of the species. But it fortifies the view that if trade explains long-distance materials transport, then such trade extended beyond both the band of 50 or so and the larger but still relatively intimate "meta-group" of 150 or so.

Migliano and Vinicius (2021) attribute a large suite of behaviors characteristic of *H. sapiens* to the "foraging niche" it came to occupy. Hominins in the human evolutionary line grew more behaviorally flexible, eating a wider variety of foods, occupying a wider variety of habitats and climates, and employing a wider variety of methods for procuring food and otherwise satisfying their needs. Behaviors characteristic of modern humans, such as cooperation with strangers, enhanced their evolutionary fitness in this ever-widening niche. Migliano and Vinicius "propose that large-scale social networks promoted the genetic, morphological and cultural evolution of modern humans by facilitating not only cultural and material exchanges but also flows of people and genes." This process of gene–culture coevolution had begun by "around" 350,000 years ago. Thus, in their theory, long-distance exchange networks had probably emerged by about 300,000 years ago and may have emerged earlier.

As far as we can tell, the existing evidence does not allow us to judge whether trade in early exchange networks was more like gift exchange or modern contractual exchange. In any event, the process of economic niche formation seems to be at least as old at the species.

We envision a primitive human ecosystem having certain roles leading to more and more specializations over time as the technospere evolves. An ecological niche is the role and the position a species has in its environment (its food and shelter needs, its survival and reproduction strategies, its function in the ecosystem, etc.). The concept of a niche as the set of ecological requirements, from the reproductive to the alimentary ones, developed by Elton (1927) and improved by Hutchinson (1957) with his definition of hypervolume, is a powerful tool for understanding the role of each species in its environment. These multidimensional spaces or hypervolumes that include all of a species' interactions with the biotic and environmental factors (traditionally labelled as abiotic, but perhaps better thought of as conbiotic on Earth [Fath and Muller 2019]), led to the consideration of niches as fundamental ecological elements able to regulate species composition and relations within an ecosystem. For example, it has been suggested that niche differences stabilize competitor dynamics by giving species higher per capita population growth rates when rare than when common, and that coexistence occurs when these stabilizing effects of niche differences overcome species in overall competitive ability (Levine and HilleRisLambers, 2009). Moreover, that nestedness of niches reduces interspecific competition and enhances the number of coexisting species (Bastolla et al., 2009).

Some authors suggested a relationship between the utilization of ecospace and change in diversity (Bambach, 1983). However, most of these previous studies emphasized the effect of niche partitioning as a global long-term pattern in the fossil record to explain the exponential diversification of life (Benton and Emerson, 2007). The main explanation for a pattern of exponential diversification is that as diversity increases, the world becomes increasingly divided into finer niche spaces. This explanation could be a result of the fact that nearly all studies of the impact of species interactions on diversification have concentrated on competition and predation, leaving out the importance of cooperative interactions (Joy, 2013). Moreover, this classical view is based on the idea that there is a preexisting ecospace (ecological niche) that is thereafter divided and partitioned, which does not take into account the unprestatable emergence of ever-new "features and functions" (Kauffman 2000, 2008, 2016, 2019), hence the new unprestatable dimensions and emergence of the new niches (Cazzolla Gatti et al. 2018). However, the idea that interactions between species are important catalysts of the evolutionary processes that generate the remarkable diversity of life is gaining interest among ecologists.

Indeed, facilitation and niche emergence (processes that allow the colonization and presence of new species taking advantage of the presence of other ones by expanding the ecosystem hypervolume) play a major role in species coexistence, strongly increasing the biodiversity of an area (Figure 8). With the

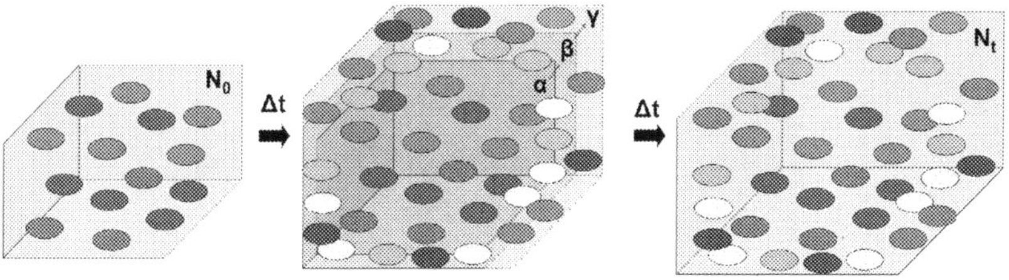

Figure 8 Niche emergence ($\alpha \rightarrow \beta \rightarrow \gamma$) is a process that allows the colonization
and presence of new species taking advantage of the presence of other ones by
expanding the ecosystem hypervolume (N_0) in an unprestatable way and,
playing a major role in species coexistence during evolutionary time (Δt),
strongly increases the biodiversity of an area (N_t).

"Biodiversity-related Niches Differentiation Theory" (BNDT), Cazzolla Gatti
(2011) proposed that species themselves are the architects of biodiversity, by
proportionally (possibly even exponentially) increasing the number of potentially
available niches in a given ecosystem. The economic parallel is that existing goods
and services are themselves available economic niches for potentially new goods
and services to enter the economy as competing to some existing goods and
completing to others (Kauffman 1988, 2008). If, as noted earlier, each new good
has more than one possible relationship as competing or completing, then it creates
more than one new economic niche and diversity explodes (Kauffman 2016, 2019).

We have also recently argued that biodiversity can be viewed as a system of
autocatalytic sets (EcoRAF sets) and that this view offers a possible answer to
the fundamental question of why so many species can coexist in the same
ecosystem (Cazzolla Gatti et al. 2017). An *autocatalytic set*, as originally
proposed by Kauffman (1986, 1993) and now defined in the context of chemistry, is a chemical reaction network in which all reactions are catalyzed by
molecules from the set itself ("reflexively autocatalytic," or RA), and all
molecules can be made from a basic food source by using only reactions from
the set itself ("food-generated," or F). Thus, an autocatalytic set has catalytic
closure (it creates its own catalysts) and is self-sustaining on a given food set
(Hordijk and Steel, 2017). An example is shown in Figure 9.

An ecological niche clearly is defined not only by the environment (in this case
the original food/resource set *F*) but also by other species and guilds that are
already present in an ecosystem (EcoRAFs), and which generate an extended
food (or resource) set. Thus, the existence of one or more species enables the
evolution and establishment of other species in the same ecosystem. In short, new
species create new niches (Figure 10). In this way, we claim that biodiversity is
autocatalytic and that increasingly diverse ecosystems are an emergent property
of evolution (EvoRAFs). Thus, diversity of species expands in a species-rich
environment, which is created by the diverse use and reuse of received energy.

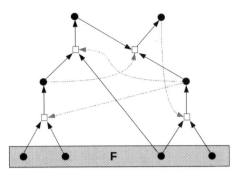

Figure 9 A simple example of an autocatalytic (RAF) set. Black dots represent molecule types, white boxes represent reactions. Solid arrows are reactants going into and products coming out of a reaction. Dashed arrows indicate which molecules catalyze which reactions. The food set F consists of the four molecule types in the gray box.

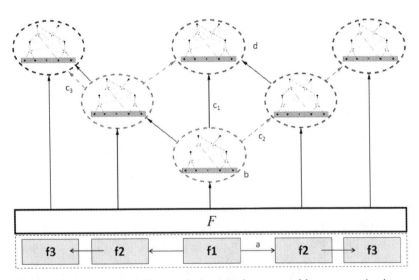

Figure 10 An example of how existing species can enable new species in an ecosystem (EcoRAF sets). Species (b), which can exist entirely on a given conditions and resources set (f1), might create some conditions and resources (f2, f3) that is required by other (potential) species catalyzing, either directly (solid arrow, c1), indirectly (dashed arrow, c2) or both (c3), thus "expanding" the conditions and resources set and enabling other species (d) to come into existence by evolutionary autocatalysis, thus creating an EvoRAFs.

In the ecological theory "niche emergence" is a neglected process, while "niche partitioning" has been widely used as a hypothesis to explain species coexistence and evolution. The emphasis put on niche (resources and conditions) partitioning for new niche evolution has hidden the reality: there is a limited possibility to prestate niches in the ecosystems because niches emerge when new species colonize the space or evolve in time (Cazzolla Gatti et al. 2018).

This provides a formal view on an evolutionary timescale. So, we have different levels of aggregation (hierarchical autocatalytic sets), which correspond to different timescales. Each set enables the (partly) unprestatable emergence of a new one. Each species, by realizing its ecological niche during the evolutionary timescale, facilitates the emergence (or the expansion) of new niches (Cazzolla Gatti et al. 2017, 2018). As Jane Jacobs (2000) observed, "the ensemble itself made the environment rich by expanding" (p. 45) as the first stage of emergence, followed by specialization and partitioning during which "an ensemble grows rich on an environment that the ensemble itself made rich" (p. 60).

An example may help clarify this theory of niche emergence. Pilot fish (*Naucrates ductor*) clean sharks' teeth. The shark opens its mouth and lets the pilot fish in. It is hard to conceive of this tooth-cleaning niche as existing, somehow, before the emergence of a relatively large swimming animal with teeth. Thus, it is inappropriate to think of this tooth-cleaning niche as the product of a subdivision of some larger, preexisting niche. Rather, the niche emerged together with shark teeth. The shark's evolutionary arrival brought with it multiple niches that cannot plausibly be thought of as existing previously. The niches created by the shark's existence are not a function of the shark alone. The existence of other species in the ecosystem creates, as it were, interaction opportunities that further multiply the number of niches created by the evolutionary arrival of sharks. The Biodiversity-related Niches Differentiation Theory (BNDT) of Cazzolla Gatti (2011) shows that the number of ecological niches in the system expands with the number of species either exponentially or as a power law. Thus, as the system evolves, the number and variety of niches ramifies and biodiversity grows. Our point is that cambiodiversity in the econosphere grows by a parallel process.

The process of niche creation may shed light on the "chicken and egg problem" discussed in Hausmann et al. (2013, 51). Crudely, I don't learn how to make automobiles because you haven't invested in distilling gasoline from petroleum. You don't learn how to distill gasoline from petroleum because I haven't invested in making automobiles. Thus, countries tend "to move into products" that use existing capabilities. "Arguably, it is easier to move from shirts to blouses than it is to move from shirts to jet engines." The theory of niche emergence clarifies that gasoline, in our example, will not be produced until there is a latent market for it.[21] In other words, something like Clower's (1965, pp. 118–120) "dual decision hypothesis" applies to the problem of bootstrapping economic development.

Autocatalytic and Emergent Economic Niches

Here, we argue that the economy can also be viewed as an autocatalytic (RAF) set, just like ecosystems, which can explain the phenomenon of niche emergence also in economic systems (Kauffman 2016, Hordijk and Steel, 2017). First, consider economic production functions as the equivalent of chemical reactions, transforming a certain number of "input" goods into a certain number of "output goods." We can model this as an evolving network, where goods are nodes on the network and directed edges the blueprint for the combinatorial production process. Networks of this type are explicated in Potts (2000) and are structures that exist at a "meso" layer between what is traditionally considered microeconomic and macroeconomic objects and interactions (Dopfer et al. 2004).

As an example of a combinatorial production network, several pieces of wood and metal can be used to produce a wheelbarrow. Next, consider the "facilitation" of such production functions as the equivalent of catalysis in chemistry. For example, a hammer can act as a "catalyst" for making wheelbarrows: it is not used up in the process, but it increases the rate at which wheelbarrows can be made. Finally, observe that the hammer itself is the product of some other production function in the same economy and that its use is not necessarily limited to making wheelbarrows. Its multifunctionality gives it many ways to contribute to new product development, thus extending its own usefulness (fitness).

In this way, an economic network forms a self-sustaining autocatalytic set: all production functions are "catalyzed" (facilitated) by-products of the same economic network, and all these products can be made from a basic set of raw materials, analogous to the food sets we discussed earlier, by using production functions from this same economic network. A simple example of an "economic RAF set," which shows emergence of economic niches, is presented in Figure 11.

In conclusion, with this novel interpretation of the economic niche and its emergence based on an ecological analysis of the autocatalytic properties of niches, we argue that diversity itself – both in ecology and economy – creates yet more diversity. In this sense, we may say that biodiversity and cambiodiversity are "autopoietic." The system is "sucked into" new opportunities. Moreover, we stated

---

[21] We thank an anonymous referee for drawing our attention to this connection and saying, "insight on niche emergence can help solve" the problem "by making clear that for innovations to occur, the existence of a latent market is indispensable."

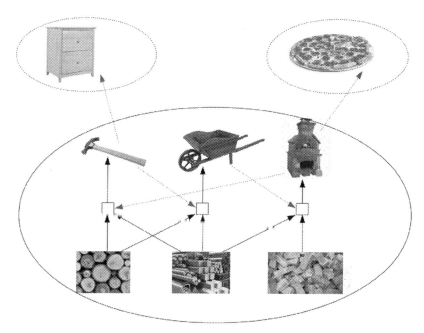

Figure 11 The main idea behind an "economic RAF set". The food set consists of wood, metal, and bricks. These can be combined in different ways to produce hammers, wheelbarrows, and brick ovens. Each of these products can also act as a catalyst: a hammer speeds up the production of wheelbarrows (without being used up in the process), the wheelbarrow speeds up the transportation of bricks to make ovens, and the oven speeds up the production of hammers by melting the metal so it can be molded into the right shape. This "economy" as a whole (within the solid oval) thus forms an autocatalytic set. Once this set is established, it may allow the emergence new "economic niches" that were not possible before (the dashed ovals).

that ecosystems in ecology and market systems in the economy are both autocatalytic sets.

In the light of this, we find that classic models of economic growth, while (of course) illuminating and important, omit an important feature of economic growth that merits closer consideration. They omit cambiodiversity and its increase over time. More traditional economic models ignore economic system autocatalysis and niche emergence. This omission is similar to the omission in most ecological models whereby, for instance, they try to predict optimum fishing strategies without taking into account that species catalyze each other's existence in autocatalytic ecosystems (Cazzolla Gatti et al. 2017) and, in this way, allow the emergence of new ecological niches available for other species (Cazzolla Gatti et al. 2018).

As we have seen, the theory of niche emergence suggests a possibly nonstandard view of the relationship between competition and cooperation. The ramification of niches allows potential competitors to occupy distinct niches between which competition is weaker or nonexistent. Ulanowicz's (2009) analysis of the "centripetality" of autocatalytic processes develops the point. The elements in an autocatalytic set move in emergent paths of self-reinforcing interdependence. But this mutualistic self-reproducing nature of the process can be disrupted by the arrival of a competitive element that draws energy or resources toward itself and away from the incumbents it is competing with. "That is, selection pressure and centripetality can guide the replacement of elements" (p. 1889). We may draw the inference that, following Ulanowicz, "competition is *subsidiary* to centripetality," which, in turn, "rests on *mutuality*" (p. 1888). If we are right to view "market competition" as autocatalytic, then the competitive element, though important and real, rests on mutuality. In other words, the "competitive market process" is first and foremost a cooperative social process.

Broadly similar views of the relationship between competition and cooperation have been expressed in the past. Smith (1776) said that "it is by treaty, by barter, and by purchase, that we obtain from one another the greater part of those mutual good offices which we stand in need of." Hayek said, "The function of competition is here precisely to teach us *who* will serve us well: which grocer or travel agency, which department store or hotel, which doctor or solicitor, we can expect to provide the most satisfactory solution for whatever particular personal problem we may have to face" (1948, p. 97, emphasis in original). Mises said, "Competing in cooperation and cooperating in competition all people are instrumental in bringing about the result" (1949, p. 335). More recently, Rubin (2019) comes much closer to our point when he says, "competition is subordinate to cooperation in an economy," even though, "there is an important role for competition." Kropotkin (1902) might at first seem to be another anticipator, at least in broad strokes. But he saw "competition" and "mutual aid" as alternatives and thought only that we rely too much on the one and too little on the other. It is our view, instead, that market competition rests, ultimately, on a logically and temporally prior mutualism among human actors.

The relationship between competition and cooperation is in part a matter of "mere semantics." But our theory of niche emergence together with Ulanowicz's analysis of mutualism and centripetality puts analytical flesh on the semantic bones of the issue. The technosphere is an autocatalytic system whose evolution produces a ramification of niches over time. The ramification of niches often allows potential competitors to move into distinct niches, thus avoiding or mitigating direct conflict of interest. Because the technosphere is an autocatalytic system, it consists of mutually supporting and reinforcing cooperative elements. Competition helps to reshape the system and to determine which parts fulfill which functions. Such competition is vital and necessary in part because of the nonmechanistic aspects of the system Ulanowicz points to. With autocatalytic systems, he explains, it is "impossible to state a priori all the possible *complex* events that could perturb an element or a relationship, much less to specify the direction in which it might move the system" (2009, p. 1889, emphasis in original). Koppl et al. (2015) say that entrepreneurs (not central planners) do the reframing Ulanowicz points to. Thus, competition is real, necessary, and salutary, but also subordinate to mutualism and cooperation. It is an aspect of mutualism and cooperation.

7 Homo Tinkerus

The tinkery quality of new combinations is a necessary consequence of the theory of the adjacent possible.[22] The elements in the adjacent possible that are available for combining are just lying around. They weren't made for each other. And because there is no deductive relation between the different uses of an object, as we discussed earlier, the consequences of combining things must be discovered. They cannot generally be deduced. Thus, combinatorial evolution proceeds by trial and error. It is tinkery business.

The notion of tinkering applies to both the evolution of the biosphere and the evolution of the technosphere. Biological evolution, François Jacob (1977, p. 1164) said, "does not produce novelties from scratch. It works on what already exists, either transforming a system to give it new functions or combining several systems to produce a more elaborate one." Jacob famously compared natural selection to "a tinkerer who does not know exactly what he is going to produce but uses whatever he finds around him whether it be pieces of string, fragments of wood or old cardboards; in short it works like a tinkerer who uses everything at his disposal to produce some kind of workable object." Solé et al. (2003) say, "the tinkerer seems to be at work" in both technology and biology. In both cases, existing elements are altered or combined with no guarantee of success.

History matters in part by determining what bits are lying about for possible recombination. Only a fraction of workable modifications and combinations are tried. And chance plays a big role in determining what modifications and combinations emerge in any period. But there is an important difference between them: Biological evolution prior to the emergence of the technosphere proceeded by metaphorical tinkering, while technological evolution proceeds by literal tinkering.

Prior to the emergence of technology with *Australopithecus afarensis*, "the tinkerer" in biological evolution was the overall system, not anyone in the system.

---

[22] Much of this section reproduces portions of Cazzolla Gatti et al. (2020).

No one imagined a biological innovation before it occurred. In the literal tinkering of technological evolution, however, "the tinkerer" is not the overall system, but an agent *within* the system. Someone *imagines* the combination before it occurs. Even when technological combinations happen by chance, as with penicillin, the chance combination cannot become a part of the ongoing technosphere without being recognized and, in this minimal sense, understood. To reproduce the winning combination, we must *imagine* ourselves purposefully combining elements that might have been first brought together by chance.

William James's (1890, p. 44) characterization of "imagination" is well suited to our purposes. "Fantasy, or Imagination, are the names given to the faculty of reproducing copies of originals once felt. The imagination is called 'reproductive' when the copies are literal; 'productive' when elements from different originals are recombined so as to make new wholes." In James's lingo, then, we may say that the technosphere has evolved through "productive imagination." Notice, however, that "imagination" so conceived is not a radical break with the past.

We have seen Alvarez, Barney, and Anderson (2013) say that technological and entrepreneurial opportunities "do not exist independently" of "perceptions." This statement exaggerates the creative power of the human mind. Combinations that have not entered the adjacent possible are generally unimaginable and, in any event, currently impossible. Combinations existing in the adjacent possible are perfectly "objective" in the sense that they exist prior to and independently of any one mind apprehending them. We also saw George Shackle (1979) describe "choosables" as "originated by the chooser." But if we are choosing merely which preexisting elements to bring together, then "choosables" are not the ex nihilo creations of an individual. They are, again, "objective" possibilities waiting to be discovered.

Bird nests, beaver dams, the elaborate mating dances of many species, and other complex artifacts and phenotypes might owe something to imagination. Perhaps. But the elaborate behavioral sequences required to produce them seem to be hard-wired into the beasts that perform them. For example, Wilsson (1971) found that European beavers (*Castor fiber L.*) would pile dam-building materials on a loudspeaker broadcasting the sound of running water or an electric razor, but not a constant tone. A central component of the beaver's dam-building program is to block up areas producing certain sounds. He says, "The beaver works to avoid variations in sound, especially the sound of flowing water" (p. 203). The United States Department of Agriculture has a publication (USDA 2005) explaining "How to keep beavers from plugging culverts." Much of the more elaborate behaviors of birds are also hard-wired. Boyd, Richerson, and Henrich (2013) say, "Birds seem to have some representation of form of the nest, but for the most part it seems that the construction process results from an algorithm which links simple, stereotypical behaviors into a sequence that generates a nest."

Mesoudi and Thornton (2018) note that some animal species have "cumulative culture evolution" in which asocial learning produces an artifact or change in behavior that spreads through "social learning," improves performance for adopters, and is modified to produce "sequential improvement over time." But their "review of the non-human literature" revealed no examples in which (1) "multiple socially learned behavioural traits are chained together to generate repeated improvement ... with each step functionally or sequentially dependent on the previous steps," (2) "parallel lineages arising when one lineage branches into multiple lineages," (3) "recombination of traits across those lineages," (4) "a trait that originally culturally evolved to maximize one performance measure [being] used to fulfil another," or (5) cultural "niche construction"[23] in which cumulative cultural evolution "modifies and creates its own selection pressures." In other words, only humans have *ramifying* cumulative cultural evolution.

Williams and Lachlan (2021), however, identify cases in which the cumulative cultural evolution of bird songs exhibits recombination and increasing complexity over time. These birds may be exercising Jamesian "productive imagination" when innovating within a song tradition. If so, however, it is a more limited form than that of humans. The more elaborate examples of nonhuman artifacts and phenotypes are, on current evidence, mostly hardwired by natural selection with at most only limited exceptions such as bird songs.

Fisher and Hinde's (1949) discussion of "[t]he opening of milk bottles by birds" illustrates the limited role of individual tinkering in animal behavior. Beginning in 1921, they explain, British tits were observed using their beaks to tear open the tops of milk bottles and drink from them. By 1949, such thieving had "become a widespread habit ... practiced by at least eleven species of birds" in parts of Great Britain and Ireland. One or a few birds learned how to do it, and the practice spread, presumably by imitation. Fisher and Hinde say, "The method of opening employed varies greatly," and "more than one method may be employed by one individual." They conclude, "It is therefore quite certain that the process which has been learnt is the whole business of obtaining milk from milk bottles, and not any particular technique for opening bottles." These avian thieves were tinkering with the lids of milk bottles. Their limited tinkering, however, did not lead to the sort of ramifying cumulative cultural evolution characteristic of the human technosphere.

Boyd, Richerson, and Henrich (2013) note the architectural quality of the "house" that *Difflugia corona* builds for itself despite having but one cell and

---

[23] Mesoudi and Thornton (2018) cite Odling-Smee, Laland, and Feldman (2003), for whom "niche construction" is the modification of an organism's environment. Birds' nests and knapped stone tools are examples. While we recognize, of course, the reality of "niche construction," we have not attempted to engage the niche construction theory of Odling, Laland, and Feldman (1996, 2003).

no central nervous system. This and other "portable protective cases" made by certain single-celled organisms (*amoebozoans* and *foraminifera*) are known as "tests" (Hansell 2011, p. R485). *Difflugia* tests are made from surrounding minerals such as silica that the organism gathers and then assembles. Hansell says *Diffulgia*'s "assembly process is probably best described as 'behavior-like' as it is wholly intracellular," but the "collection of the building material is a more obviously behavioral process" (2011, p. R486). Figure 12a shows the test of a *Difflugia urceolata*. Figure 12b shows a living foraminifera, *Heterostegina depressa*. It is 3.5 mm across, which is the size of a standard audio jack such as that on an iPhone 5 (Boudagher-Fadel 2018 Plate 1.3 p. 41).

The elaborate "tests" Foraminifera construct for themselves led one observer to impute "purposive intelligence" to them (Heron-Allen 1915, p. 555). We instead find in them evidence to support our conjecture that the sort of imaginative tinkering we impute to humans made little or no contribution to biological evolution prior to the emergence of the human technosphere, where it is of the highest importance.

The biological tinkerer was metaphorical, we have said, "prior to the emergence of technology with *Australopithecus afarensis*." But we do not feel able to judge whether australopithecine knappers were literal tinkerers. They may

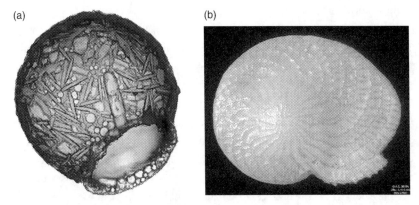

(a)   (b)

Figure 12a A test built by *Difflugia corona*. Alain Couette, CC BY-SA 3.0, via Wikimedia Commons

12b A test built by *Heterostegina depressa*. Rothaus, CC BY-SA 4.0, via Wikimedia Commons

have been. But the Acheulean technology, which predominated from over a million years[24] ago to about 500,000 years ago, might have been genetically

---

[24] One textbook says, Acheulean technology "first appears in the archaeological record at 1.4 mya (newer data suggests possibly as early as 1.7 mya) and lasted to as late as 115 kya in some areas" (Welker 2017, p. 170). Leader et al. (2018) may be the "recent result" Welker

rather than culturally transmitted (Shipton and Neilson 2018). If so, it is unlikely that Acheulian and earlier technologies were the product of imaginative individual tinkering. It would then be a fair guess that individual tinkering may have begun only about the time of the emergence of composite tools 500,000 years ago or even, perhaps, later. Paraphrasing Bergstrom et al. (2021, p. 231), however, it is not conceptually meaningful to describe the time depth of the cognitive apparatus of early modern humans with point estimates.

There was no precise moment when something we may call "tinkering" leapt into being and grabbed hold of hominin toolmaking. But we do have good evidence of individual tinkering from about the emergence of composite tools and the correlated "Levallois" stone technology. Tryon, McBrearty, and Texier (2005) experimented with reproducing Levallois flakes. They found that "it is necessary to use a range of hammerstones of different weights and textures for the production of a single large Levallois flake, according to the variable circumstances and kind of core preparation locally required" (p. 212). Wadley (2016, p. 60) reports that adhesives made in Sibudu Cave (in present-day South Africa) at least 70,000 years ago required improvisation. "The plasticity of plant gum, the aggregate-size of ground iron oxides and the heat of fires are inconsistent natural features that require a slightly different recipe and processing procedure for each adhesive manufacturing event." Such unscripted adjustments are tinkering. Presumably, these unscripted adjustments were required from the earliest emergence of composite tools. Shimelmitz and Kuhn (2018) emphasize the variety of shapes produced in the "Levallois" technology that emerged with composite tools. They rebuff the view that Levallois technology was a rigid program that produced a few archetypal tools. Stone knappers were not lashed to "arbitrary, culturally dictated" procedures, they say. Rather, "variation in Levallois technology may also reflect behavioral responses to different economic contingencies and constraints." The procedural flexibility, "large number of variants," and reshaping of bits that archaeologists once viewed as waste all support the idea that the makers of composite tools were tinkering their way along right from the start.

Reason and foresight have played a smaller role in the evolution of the technosphere than many popular and scientific accounts suggest. We believe Nelson and Nelson (2002) were right to speak of the "necessity," when explaining technology, "of setting human knowledge into the biological evolutionary framework congruent with that of other animals, where the point is to learn about and adapt within the world," while also incorporating the "special human

---

refers to. Gibbon et al. (2009) gave one sample of Aucheulean stone tools a maximum age of 1.89 ± 0.19 million years and a minimum age of 1.72 ± 0.16 million years. Leader et al. (2018), however, revised that range to maximum age of 1.73 ± 0.16 million years and a minimum age of 1.67 ± 0.16 million years.

capacities for symbolic communication and collective problem-solving" (p. 725). Insight and serendipity mingle and combine in their analysis. Even in the most science-heavy fields, "technological advance remains somewhat blind" because tinkering technologists are trying to reach beyond the grasp of current science. "Thus, while radio communication clearly would have been impossible without Maxwell's theorizing and Hertz' critical experiments and demonstrations, the development of an effective means of radio communication required a great deal of trial and feedback effort by inventors and engineers."

In some cases, useful combination will be fortuitous as the histories of penicillin and Post-it notes may help to suggest. In others, the element of planful search may be larger. The Wright brothers, for example, were trying to make a workable airplane. And they had a fairly clear idea of what elements needed combining. (The main elements were an airfoil, a light gas engine, bicycle wheels, and a propeller.) But the element of tinkering in their efforts was by no means absent (Ridley 2020, pp. 95–103 and 253). Pure reason was insufficient to reach the precise combination that would sustain flight. And even today, there are two main competing scientific explanations of lift and no scientific consensus, leading one writer to declare, "No One Can Explain Why Planes Stay In The Air" (Regis 2020).

Technology evolves when tinkering humans cobble together existing elements. If "thinking" is something close to standard economic "rationality" and if the evolution of the technosphere is governed by a process that emerged prior to modern humans, then "thinking" may play a smaller role than tinkering in the evolution of the technosphere. Technological progress comes not from some Socratic thinkery, but from a Darwinian tinkery.

If progress comes from tinkering, not thinking, then we may justly speak of "*Homo tinkerus*." Jacob (1977) suggests the metaphor of evolution as tinkerer as we have noted earlier. Kauffman (2019) has used the term "jury-rigging." Levi-Strauss (1966) used the roughly equivalent term "bricolage," which has gained currency in management and entrepreneurship (Weick 1993, Garud and Karnøe 2003, Baker and Nelson 2005) and in law (Hull 1991 p. 317, Meyer 2014, Timmer 2015 p. 275). The words "tinkering" and "bricolage" are often used interchangeably. But some aspects of Levi-Strauss's original characterization of "bricolage" may be inappropriate for our theory of technological change. The "bricoleur," Levi-Strauss tells us, "is adept at performing a large number of diverse tasks," their "universe of instruments is closed" and "bears no relation to the current project." Their tools are only things that "may always come in handy" (pp. 17–18). Thus, the word "bricolage" may have some tendency to inappropriately suggest a lack of specialization and even an aversion to novelty, whereas the most "rational," planful, and advanced specialists in any technological domain are tinkerers.

When considering technological change, we should model humans as tinkerers, cobbling together existing elements as well as they can, adjusting, tweaking, and combining in an unending process of trial and error. Technological change is not so much the product of reason, intelligence, and foresight as of tinkering and improvisation. To be sure, only a creature that is highly intelligent by biological standards could perform the required tinkering. *Homo tinkerus* must *understand* the domain in which they tinker. (We thank Brian Arthur for impressing this point upon us in correspondence.) Thus, while tinkering does not match the model of rational search in standard economics, it does require the sort of conscious intelligence traditionally thought to exist only in humans. Thus, tinkering is not *completely* random, ad hoc, or arbitrary notwithstanding the random, ad hoc, and arbitrary elements in it. Instead, tinkering is generally aimed at filling recently emergent possibilities, as we develop shortly in our discussion of economic niches. The Wright brothers were *trying* to achieve heavier-than-air-powered flight. But, as we have noted, they did not so much design their way there as tinker their way there. And they could not have gotten on the right path until the relevant technological possibilities had opened up, which is to say that both gliders and internal combustion engines had to exist before the Wright brothers and others could begin experimenting with ways to cobble them together.

Our tinkery vision of technological progress may seem less surprising if we recognize the importance of tinkering in research science. Knorr (1979, p. 350) insists that "the mechanisms ruling the progress of research are more adequately described as successful 'tinkering' rather than as hypothesis testing or cumulative verification." Biologist Kenneth Norris (1993, p. 107) says, "Science is tinkery business." Kantorovich (1993, p. 3) argued that tinkering "is part and parcel of the very nature of scientific discovery and human creativity in general."

Jamesian "productive imagination" operates on "copies of originals once felt." The imaginative actor is manipulating preexisting categories. Thus, a preexisting category, concept, or image is required for "chance" phenomena to be observed. The point here is close to Kant's point that "a priori" categories organize experience. In Kant, such categories are universal and necessary. "Necessity and strict universality, therefore, are infallible tests for distinguishing pure from empirical knowledge, and are inseparably connected with each other" (Kant 1787, p. 26 [section II of "Introduction"]). For other authors, however, such "a priori" categories need not be necessary or universal. In Hayek (1952) the categories are mutable and emerge from both biological evolution and personal experience.

"Attention," Hayek says, is "always directed, or confined to a particular class of events for which we are on the look-out" (1952, p. 139).[25]

Felin et al. (2018, p. 816) have a helpful discussion of Uexküll's (1934) related notion of "*Suchbild*" or "search image." They explain, "It is this *Suchbild* that directs perception toward the awareness of, generation, and finding of certain cues, such as relevant objects or, say, sources of food. For example, many species of frog will not recognize a fly directly in front of them unless it moves."[26] Objects made salient by one's *Suchbild* are candidates for recombination or modification. Without an enabling *Suchbild*, it is unlikely or impossible for objects to be combined.

These considerations give us an economic "theory of ideas," though we do not intend to comment on the vast philosophical literature that also goes under this heading. In a broad sense, our theory assumes "bounded rationality." But we follow Felin et al. (2017) in rejecting the "all-seeing eye" of Simon (1955b), Kahneman (2003), and others. Our model is closer to those of Smith (2009), Koppl (2018), Rizzo and Whitman (2020), and especially Felin et al. (2017). While our theory is not tied to Uexküll, his language is convenient for us, in part because of the important work of Felin et al. (2017) and Felin et al. (2018) which builds on Uexküll. Our theory can be sketched in four points.

(1) Tinkering entrepreneurs are guided by their preexisting *Suchbilden*.

(2) Human *Suchbilden* and *Umwelten* change within generations, whereas for many other species they can change only between generations through genetic change. Presumably, there is something of a continuum between the rigidity of the *E. coli*'s *Umwelt* and the plasticity of *H. sapiens*' many *Umwelten*.

(3) Human *Suchbilden* render human entrepreneurs alert to new combinations. The general, though not universal, rule is that nonhuman animals don't

---

[25] We have suppressed Hayek's footnote, "Cf., W. Stern, 1938, p. 474." Hayek may have been referring in part to Stern's comment, "During an act of attention consciousness possesses a peculiar dual alertness for both that which is given presently and that which is next expected."

[26] We endorse Uexküll's subjectivism, but not his anti-Darwinism, his one-sided emphasis on the supposed harmony of nature, or his injection into science of "an all-encompassing plan" (1934, p. 200) of the universe. Uexküll (1934, p. 183) invokes "the higher unity of the species" to immunize his view of nature as a harmonious symphony from the otherwise destructive implications of conflict and cruelty in nature. "In order to maintain the species at the same number of individuals," Uexküll says, "the surplus ones must go under." Without this arbitrary introduction of design to his system of ideas, the symphony of nature descends from harmony to dissonance and discord. Nature again appears red in tooth and claw. Only a higher being with "an all-encompassing plan" could act to keep membership in each species at a constant level. But the hypothesis of such constancy is false, with some species growing in numbers, other shrinking, and still other fluctuating in irregular ups and downs. Ulanowicz's (2009) notion of "centripetality," discussed earlier, softens the view of nature as red in tooth and claw, but does displace it. The idea of centripetality does not rely on an evolutionary teleology or any notion of an overarching plan; it retains natural selection and competition.

make new combinations within generations; it takes genetic change to induce a new combination. That general rule has exceptions, as we have seen. But other species seem to have lower capacities for cross-generational learning. Partly for this reason, when other animals learn a new trick within a generation, it does not form a cumulative process that is as elaborate as the evolution of the human technosphere.

(4) Humans can *imagine* new combinations. Our imagination is not ex nihilo creation, but just discovering what existing elements might be combined usefully. But precisely because there is no deductive relationship between combinations and effects, we must also *discover* the causal consequences of new combinations, which implies tinkering. On the one hand, we learn what is out there to combine. On the other hand, we cannot confidently predict the consequences of any imagined combination. Thus, trial and error, tinkering, and openness to chance events are required to cobble onto good, new, workable combinations.

8 Entrepreneurship and Innovation

Our tinkery theory of technological change should probably be seen as supportive of Israel Kirzner's theory of entrepreneurship (Kirzner 1973, 1982, 1997).[27] Kirzner has been the great advocate of "opportunity discovery." The theory of the adjacent possible redeems Kirzner's basic insight. In Kirzner's theory, entrepreneurship consists in perceiving a new and better ends-means framework. The difficulty has always been where opportunities come from. And it must be admitted that Kirzner did not give a clear and consistent answer to this question. The theory of the adjacent possible shows that opportunities are created by the system, rather than being some sort of ex nihilo creation of individual brains. At any moment, the potential combinations in the adjacent possible exist independently of the entrepreneur who "merely" *discovers* one or more of these preexisting combinations.

We may unpack this process with the conceptual apparatus of "alertness," "opportunity," and "discovery." A robot cannot perceive a new ends-means framework. It cannot "really" learn. It can update as new information arrives, but only in strict accordance with the algorithms – the basic analytical framework – programmed into it. Humans learn in a much more radical sense. They change the analytical framework shaping their choices. This disposition to learn is called "alertness" in Kirzner's theory. There has been "discovery" when something is learned that changes a person's ends-means framework. And because discovery

---

27 Much of this section reproduces portions of Cazzolla Gatti et al. (2020).

changes the ends-means framework, it is always and necessarily discovery of an opportunity. It is an opportunity because it represents improvement or gain. It represents, in other words, *profit* in the most general sense of the word. An opportunity *is* a profit opportunity. Of course, this profit exists ex ante and not necessarily ex post. The new plan may not work out. As Kirzner has said, "viewed ex ante, every entrepreneurial decision taken envisages *only* profit" (1973, p. 83). The entrepreneur will generally know perfectly well that they are taking a risk. No special insight is required to know that life is full of surprises, not all of them happy. But if the action is taken, then the prospective gain outweighed the potential loss and entrepreneurial opportunity represented an ex ante profit. Bringing the pieces together, we may say that the *alert* entrepreneur *discovers* an *opportunity* to change their *ends-means* framework, thereby gaining an (*ex ante*) *profit*.

It is a perennial question in the entrepreneurship literature whether the entre-preneurial opportunities are "objective" (Shane and Venkantaraman 2000, McMullen and Shepherd 2006, Alvarez, Barney, and Anderson 2013, Ramoglou 2021, McBride and Wuebker 2022). One might say (as at least some of us do) that the opportunities are "objective" because the elements that might be combined exist in the adjacent possible. For such a combination to be realized, however, it must first be imagined. And some persons will insist that the act of Jamesian imagination required for a Kirznerian "discovery" makes the opportun-ity "subjective." Foss and Klein (2012, 2020) seem to say that uncertainty implies opportunities cannot be construed as externally existing in some objective sense. "Profit," they say, "is a reward to bearing uncertainty, specifically a return that accrues to those entrepreneurs who are particularly optimistic in the face of ambiguity and who succeed with their entrepreneurial ventures" (p. 96). Thus, they view profit as ex post. We prefer, with Kirzner, to view profit as ex ante.

Vocabulary is less important than one's substantive position. In our view, the creativity of the economic system is a matter of recombination. And new combinatorial possibilities emerge through the evolution of the system rather than as exogenous thoughts of entrepreneurs. In everyday language we say Thomas Edison and Steve Jobs were "creative." But their "creativity" consisted in combining preexisting elements already present in the adjacent possible.

Our basic conceptual framework for entrepreneurship – which we attribute to Kirzner – is applicable to every human action. It is applicable to every action because the entrepreneurial element is present in all human action (Koppl and Minniti 2010). Entrepreneurship is a human universal. The phenomenon of opportunity discovery is always present despite the many potentially confound-ing particulars of the real world. While entrepreneurship scholars still debate the nature of entrepreneurial opportunities, the general understanding of entrepreneurial opportunity that we have briefly sketched lets scholars examine more complicated phenomena without risking confusion and incoherence.

Our perspective on entrepreneurship might be loosely characterized as "Darwinizing Kirzner." And this perspective fits nicely with a kind of vision statement found in Foster (2021 p. 16). Foster says, "economic change is the result of creativity and cooperation." Humans get along "not just by observing the world around them, but by constructing new knowledge, via the imagination." We endorse this view, albeit with the caveat that "imagination" is William James' "faculty of reproducing copies of originals once felt" (1890, p. 44). This caveat makes "creativity" a property of the system as a whole rather than individual agents within the system. For Foster, "economic self-organisation is the primary driver of economic evolution. Such a heuristic has a solid evidential basis in the vast number of case studies of entrepreneurship and innovation." He cautions us, however, that "a heuristic is only of scientific value if it can be directly connected to an empirical methodology that can address historical data that economic systems generate." Our tinkery vision of technological evolution seems to fit Foster's vision. And our "tri-data result" connects theory and history in much the way Foster seems to call for.

9 Coda

We began our story with *Australopithecus afarensis* and the first knapped stone tools. We have seen that *Homo sapiens* and the technosphere have coevolved and that this coevolutionary process began before the emergence of genus *Homo*. We have seen that the combinatorial process of technological change was fundamentally unchanged for at least the past 500,000 years and perhaps the past 3.3 million years. And we have seen that the parameters of the TAP process (P and the α_i values) have been stable for the last 2,000 years and may have been stable for about the last 100,000 years. The technosphere evolved with us and not apart from us. It is not apart *from* nature, but a part *of* nature.

If our explanation of technology is about right, then we should not view technology as somehow unnatural or apart from nature. Rather, it is one of the more spectacular and bizarre products of the evolution of life on earth. We are a part of nature not only because we share an evolutionary history with all terrestrial life forms, but also because the technosphere, our technosphere, is a part of nature. The technosphere was not designed by any rational, godlike creature, standing apart from the surge and flux of earthly life. It emerged unintendedly from the tinkering, testing, and trying of creatures but little wiser than their primate cousins.

Appendix

Our opening paragraph dates the origin of the human technosphere to 3.3 million years ago and the origin of *H. sapiens* to 315,000 years ago. These dates imply that the history of technology began an order of magnitude longer than the history of the species (since 3.3 million is about 10.48 times greater than 315,000). But there are, of course, ambiguities in dating both the origin of the technosphere and the origin of our species.

It is possible that the tools discussed in Harmand et al. (2015), the "Lomekwi 3" or "LOM3" tools, represent neither the origin of the modern human technosphere nor an early stage in its evolution. Harmand et al. (2015) and Lewis and Harmand (2016) both allow for the possibility that the 3.3-million-year-old knapped tools may have been made by the hominin species *Kenyanthropus platyops*. If *K. platyops* manufactured the LOM3 tools but was not an ancestor of modern humans, then the earliest known knapped stone tools in the continuous history of the technosphere would be Oldowan tools, which emerged about 2.6 million years ago. In this case, the origin of the technosphere still greatly precedes the emergence of *H. sapiens*.

Without choosing between *A. afarensis* and *K. platyops*, either of which might be an ancestral species of ours, Lewis and Harmand (2016) think the LOM3 tools were probably manufactured by "our ancestors." Harmand et al. (2015) hint that the LOM3 tools are more likely to have been made by *A. afarensis* than *K. platyops* when they note that McPherron et al. (2010) found evidence that stone tools were used by *A. afarensis* to cut the flesh from bones about 3.39 million years ago. Fuentes (2019) notes that *A. afarensis*, *K. platyops*, and *Australopithecus deyiremeda* are all candidates for the makers of the LOM3 tools. (The possibility that *A. deyiremeda* made the LOM3 tools is the most remote of the three possibilities.) He says, however, that it is "most likely" that they were made by *A. afarensis*. We have ignored the possibility that the LOM3 tools were not produced by "our ancestors," and we have assumed those ancestors were *A. afarensis*. But our overall argument is little affected by the possibility that the LOM3 tools are not the origin of the modern technosphere. The modern human technosphere clearly shares an evolutionary history with Oldowan tools, which emerged about 2.6 million years ago and thus long before the emergence of *H. sapiens*. Thus, even in the unlikely event that the LOM3 tools must be cast out from the history of the human technosphere, that history requires a broadly Darwinian perspective.

The ratio of the history of technology to the history of the species is not much changed if we adjust the assumed emergence of biologically modern humans to the most distant date consistent with current best evidence and adjust the assumed beginning of human technology to the most recent date consistent with current best evidence.

Hublin et al. (2017) found remains they classify as *Homo sapiens* and date to "315 ± 34 thousand years" (p. 289). If we imagine that the species began at the most distant extreme of this range, it emerged at least 349,000 years ago. Schlebusch et al. (2017) find evidence that *H. sapiens* separated off from other hominins between 350,000 and 260,000 years ago. Harmand et al. (2015) found their tools in a stratum of earth dating from 3.33 to 3.21 million years ago. They are quite clear that the 3.21 value is too recent for their tools and offer the 3.3 value as a precise value. We nevertheless note that 3.21 million is about 9.2 times greater than 350,000, which is close to an order of magnitude. It is unlikely, however, that very earliest knapped stone tools actually used were those found by Harmand et al. (2015). Recall that McPherron et al. (2010) find evidence that stone tools were used to cut the flesh from bones about 3.39 million years ago, but without finding the tools themselves. They say, "It is not possible to demonstrate from the modified bones whether the stone tools were knapped for this purpose or whether naturally occurring sharp-edged stones were collected and used." Thus, the continuous history of human technology may have already begun by 3.39 million years ago. And it is reasonable to guess that even earlier tools may have been crafted from wood or other organic materials that would be less likely than stone tools to survive to the present in a form recognizable as a tool.

It is also unsure whether we should concur in the judgment of Hublin et al. (2017) that the remains they found should be considered *Homo sapiens*. Bergstrom et al. (2021) object that the Hublin et al. specimens "lack a globular cranial vault" and are thus dissimilar to present-day humans. They suggest that *Homo sapiens* may have emerged only about 150,000 years ago, while maintaining a salutary vagueness about just how early *H. sapiens* may have arrived. And, as they note, dating the emergence of the species is an inherently ambiguous project. They say, "it is not conceptually meaningful to describe the time depth of the population structure of early modern humans with point estimates" (Bergstrom et al. 2021, p. 231).

Overall, it is probably an understatement and at worst a serviceable approximation to say that the history of technology is an order of magnitude longer than the history of biologically modern humans.

References

Aiello, L. C., and Dunbar, R. I. M. 1993. "Neocortex size, group size, and the evolution of language." *Current Anthropology*, 34(2): 184–193.

Aldrich, H., Hodgson, G., Hull, D. et al. 2008. "In defence of generalised Darwinism." *Journal of Evolutionary Economics*, 18(5): 577–596.

Almudi, I., and Fatas-Villafranca, F. 2021. *Coevolution in Economic Systems*. Cambridge: Cambridge University Press.

Alvarez, S. A., Barney, J. B., and Anderson, P. 2013. "Forming and exploiting opportunities: The implications of discovery and creation processes for entrepreneurial and organizational research." *Organization Science*, 24(1): 301–317.

Álvarez-Nogal, C., and Prados de la Escosura, L. 2013. "The rise and fall of Spain (1270–1850)." *Economic History Review*, 66: 1–37.

Ambrose, S. H. 2001. "Paleolithic technology and human evolution." *Science*, 291: 1748–1753.

Arifovic, J., Bullard, J., and Duffy, J. 1997. "The transition from stagnation to growth: An adaptive learning approach." *Journal of Economic Growth*, 2: 185–209.

Arthur, W. B. 1994. "Inductive reasoning and bounded rationality." *American Economic Review: Papers and Proceedings*, 84: 406–411.

Arthur, W. B. 2007. "The structure of invention." *Research Policy*, 36(2): 274–287.

Arthur, W. B. 2009. *The Nature of Technology: What It Is and How It Evolves*. New York: Free Press.

Arthur, W. B., and Polak, W. 2006. "The evolution of technology within a simple computer model." *Complexity*, 11(5): 23–31.

Baker, T., and Nelson, R. 2005. "Creating something from nothing: Resource construction through entrepreneurial bricolage." *Administrative Science Quarterly*, 50(3): 329–366.

Bambach, R. K. 1983. "Ecospace utilization and guilds in marine communities through the Phanerozoic." In M. J. S. Tevesz and P. L. McCall (eds.), *Biotic Interactions in Recent and Fossil Benthic Communities*. Boston, MA: Springer, pp. 719–746.

Barkow, J. H., Cosmides, L., and Tooby, J. (eds.). 1992. *The Adapted Mind: Evolutionary Psychology and the Generation of Culture*. New York: Oxford University Press.

Bastolla, U., Fortuna, M. A., Pascual-García, A. et al. 2009. "The architecture of mutualistic networks minimizes competition and increases biodiversity." *Nature*, 458(7241): 1018–1020.

Bedau, M. A. 2014. "Testing bottom-up models of complex citation networks." *Philosophy of Science*, 81(5): 1131–1143.

Beinhocker, E. D. 2006. *The Origin of Wealth: Evolution, Complexity, and the Radical Remaking of Economics*. Cambridge, MA: Harvard Business Review Press.

Beinhocker, E. D. 2011. "Evolution as computation: Integrating self-organization with generalized Darwinism." *Journal of Institutional Economics*, 7(3): 393–423.

Bentley, A. R., Hahn, M. W., and Shennan, S. J. 2004. "Random drift and culture change." *Proceedings: Biological Sciences*, 271(1547): 1443–1450.

Benton, M. J., and Emerson, B. C. 2007. "How did life become so diverse? The dynamics of diversification according to the fossil record and molecular phylogenetics." *Palaeontology*, 50(1): 23–40.

Bergstrom, A., Stringer, C., Hajdinjak, M., Scerri, E. M. L., and Skoglund, P. 2021. "Origins of modern human ancestry." *Nature*, 590: 229–237.

Blegen, N. 2017. "The earliest long-distance obsidian transport: Evidence from the ~200 ka Middle Stone Age Sibilo School Road Site, Baringo, Kenya." *Journal of Human Evolution*, 103: 1–19.

Blegen, N., Jicha, B. R., and McBrearty, S. 2018. "A new tephrochronology for early diverse stone tool technologies and long-distance raw material transport in the Middle to Late Pleistocene Kapthurin Formation, East Africa." *Journal of Human Evolution*, 121: 75–103.

Boudagher-Fadel, M. K. 2018. "Biology and evolutionary history of larger benthic foraminifera." In M. K. Boudagher-Fadel, *Evolution and Geological Significance of Larger Benthic Foraminifera*, 2nd ed. London: UCL Press, pp. 1–44. DOI: https://doi.org/10.2307/j.ctvqhsq3.3.

Boyd, R., and Richerson, P. J. 1985. *Culture and the Evolutionary Process*. Chicago: The University of Chicago Press.

Boyd, R., and Richerson, P. J. 2021. "Large-scale cooperation in small-scale foraging societies." EcoEvoRxiv. May 17. DOI: https://doi.org/10.32942/osf.io/fxwbr.

Boyd, R., Richerson, P. J., and Henrich, J. 2013. "The cultural evolution of technology: Facts and theory." In P. J. Richerson and M. H. Christiansen (eds.), *Cultural Evolution: Society, Technology, Language, and Religion*. Cambridge, MA: Massachusetts Institute of Technology Press, pp. 119–142.

Broadberry, S., Campbell, B., Klein, A., Overton, M., and van Leeuwen, B. 2015. *British Economic Growth: 1270–1870*. Cambridge: Cambridge University Press.

Brooks, A. S., Yellen, J. E., Potts, R. et al. 2018. "Long-distance stone transport and pigment use in the earliest Middle Stone Age." *Science*, 360: 90–94.

Campbell, D. T. 1965. "Variation and selective retention in socio-cultural evolution." In H. R. Barringer, G. I. Blanksten, and R. W. Mack (eds.), *Social Change in Developing Areas: A Reinterpretation of Evolutionary Theory.* Cambridge, MA: Schenkman Publishing Company, pp. 19–49.

Cazzolla Gatti, R. 2011. "Evolution is a cooperative process: The biodiversity-related niches differentiation theory (BNDT) can explain why." *Theoretical Biology Forum*, 104(1): 35–43.

Cazzolla Gatti, R., Fath, B., Hordijk, W., Kauffman, S., and Ulanowicz, R. 2018. "Niche emergence as an autocatalytic process in the evolution of ecosystems." *Journal of Theoretical Biology*, 454: 110–117.

Cazzolla Gatti, R., Hordijk, W., and Kauffman, S. (2017). "Biodiversity is autocatalytic." *Ecological Modelling*, 346: 70–76.

Cazzolla Gatti, R., Koppl, R., Fath, B. et al. 2020. "On the emergence of ecological and economic niches." *Journal of Bioeconomics*, 22(2): 99–127.

Chaitin, G., da Costa, N., and Doria, F. A. 2012. *Gödel's Way: Exploits into an Undecidable World.* Boca Raton, FL: CRC Press.

Chen, C., and Hicks, D. 2004. "Tracing knowledge diffusion." *Scientometrics*, 59(2): 199–211.

Clark, G. 2007. *A Farewell to Alms: A Brief Economic History of the World.* Princeton, NJ: Princeton University Press.

Clark, R. W. 1985. *The Life of Ernst Chain: Penicillin and Beyond.* New York: St. Martin's Press.

Clower, R. W. 1965. "The Keynesian counter-revolution: A theoretical appraisal." In F. H. Hahn and F. P. R. Brechling (eds.), *The Theory of Interest Rates.* London: Macmillan, pp. 103–125.

Cohen, W. M., and Levinthal, D. A. 1990. "Absorptive capacity: A new perspective on learning and innovation." *Administrative Science Quarterly*, 35(1):128–152.

Comin, D., and Hobijn, B. 2010. "An exploration of technology diffusion." *American Economic Review*, 100, 2031–2059. DOI:https://doi.org/10.1257/aer .100.5.2031.

Conway, M. S. 2006. "Darwin's dilemma: The realities of the Cambrian 'explosion'." *Philosophical Transactions of the Royal Society B: Biological Sciences*, 361(1470): 1069–1083.

Cortês, M., Kauffman, S. A., Liddle, A. R. and Smolin, L. "The TAP equation: evaluating combinatorial innovation," *arXiv:2204.14115*.

Crafts, N. F. R. 1977. "Industrial Revolution in England and France: Some thoughts on the question, 'Why was England first?'" *The Economic History Review*, 30(3): 429–441.

da Costa, N. C. A., and Doria, F. A. 1991. "Undecidability and incompleteness in classical mechanics." *International Journal of Theoretical Physics*, 30: 1041–1073.

Dam, K. W. *The Law-Growth Nexus: The Rule of Law and Economic Development*. Washington: Brookings Institution Press, 2005.

Debreu, G. 1959. *Theory of Value*. New Haven, CT: Yale University Press.

Deino, A. L. et al. 2018. "Chronology of the Acheulean to Middle Stone Age transition in eastern Africa." *Science*, 360: 95–98.

Devereaux, A., Koppl, R., Kauffman, S., and Roli A. 2021. "An incompleteness result regarding within-system modeling." SSRN 3968077.

Domínguez-Rodrigo, M., Cobo-Sánchez, L., Aramendi, J., and Gidna, A. 2019. "The meta-group social network of early humans: A temporal-spatial assessment of group size at FLK Zinj (Olduvai Gorge, Tanzania)." *Journal of Human Evolution*, 127: 54–66.

Dopfer, K., Foster, J., and Potts, J. 2004. "Micro-meso-macro." *Journal of Evolutionary Economics*, 14(3): 263–279. DOI: https://doi.org/10.1007/s00191-004-0193-0.

Dunbar, R. I. M. 1992. "Neocortex size as a constraint on group size in primates." *Journal of Human Evolution*, 20: 469–493.

Dunbar, R. I. M. 1998. "The social brain hypothesis." *Evolutionary Anthropology: Issues, News, and Reviews*, 6(5): 178–190.

Dunbar, R. I. M. 2020. "Structure and function in human and primate social networks: Implications for diffusion, network stability and health." *Proceedings of the Royal Society A*, 476: 20200446.

Dunbar, R. I. M. 2021. *Friends: Understanding the Power of Our Most Important Relationships*. London: Little, Brown.

Dutta, R. D. K., Levine, N. W., and Papageorge, L. W. 2018. "Entertaining Malthus, circuses, and economic growth." *Economic Inquiry*, 56: 358–380.

Enkel E., Groemminger, A., and Heil, S. 2018. "Managing technological distance in internal and external collaborations: Absorptive capacity routines and social integration for innovation." *Journal of Technology Transfer*, 43(5): 1257–1290.

Elton, C. S. 1927. *Animal Ecology*. Chicago: University of Chicago Press.

Estoup, J. B. 1916. *Gammes Stenographiques*. Paris: Institut Stenographique de France.

Fath, B. D. 2007. "Network mutualism: Positive community level relations in ecosystems." *Ecological Modelling*, 208: 56–67.

Fath, B. D., and Müller, F. 2019. "Conbiota." In B. D. Fath (ed.), *Encyclopedia of Ecology* (2nd ed.), pp. 274–280.

Felin, T., Koenderink, J., and Krueger, J. 2017. "Rationality, perception, and the all-seeing eye." *Psychonomic Bulletin & Review*, 24: 1040–1059.

Felin, T., Koenderink, J., and Krueger, J. 2018. "Cues, minds, and equilibria: Responses and extenstions." *Psychonomic Bulletin & Review*, 25: 813–826.

Fink, T. M. A., and Reeves, M. 2019. "How much can we influence the rate of innovation?" *Science Advances*, 5(1): eaat6107.

Fink, T. M. A., Reeves, M., Palma, R., and Farr, R. S. 2017. "Serendipity and strategy in rapid innovation." *Nature Communications*, 8(1): 2002.

Fisher, J., and Hinde, R. A. (1949). "The opening of milk bottles by birds." *British Birds*, 42: 347–357.

Fleming, A. 1929. "On the antibacterial action of cultures of a penicillium, with special reference to their use in the isolation of *B. influenzae*." *The British Journal of Experimental Pathology*, 10: 226–236. (Reprinted in *Reviews of Infectious Diseases*, 1980, 2(1): 129–139.)

Fleming, L., and Sorenson, O. 2001. "Technology as a complex adaptive system: Evidence from patent data." *Research Policy*, 30: 1019–1039.

Foss, N. J., and Klein, P. G. 2012. *Organizing Entrepreneurial Judgment.* Cambridge University Press.

Foss, N. J., and Klein, P. G. 2020. "Entrepreneurial opportunities: Who needs them?" *Academy of Management Perspectives*, 34: 366–377.

Foster, J. 2021. "In search of a suitable heuristic for evolutionary economics: From generalized Darwinism to economic self-organisation," MPRA Paper No. 106146. Online at https://mpra.ub.uni-muenchen.de/106146/.

Galor, O., and Weil, D. N. 2000. "Population, technology, and growth: From Malthusian stagnation to the demographic transition and beyond." *American Economic Review*, 90: 806–828.

Garud, R., and Karnøe, P. 2003. "Bricolage versus breakthrough: Distributed and embedded agency in technology entrepreneurship." *Research Policy*, 32: 277–300.

Gibbon, R. J., Ganger, D. E., Kuman, K., and Partridge, T. C. 2009. "Early Acheulean technology in the Rietputs Formation, South Africa, dated with cosmogenic nuclides." *Journal of Human Evolution*, 56: 152–160.

Gilsing, V., Nooteboom, B., Vanhaverbeke, W., Duysters, G., and van den Oord, Ad. 2008. "Network embeddedness and the exploration of novel technologies: Technological distance, betweenness centrality and density." *Research Policy*, 37: 1717–1731.

Golan, O., and Moav, O. 2002. "Natural selection and the origin of economic growth." *The Quarterly Journal of Economics*, 67(4): 1133–1191.

Goldstone, J. A. 2002. "Efflorescences and economic growth in world history: Rethinking the 'rise of the West' and the Industrial Revolution." *Journal of World History*, 13(2): 323–389.

Goren-Inbar, N., and Belfer-Cohen, A. 2020. "Reappraisal of hominin group size in the Lower Paleolithic: An introduction to the special issue." *Journal of Human Evolution*, 144: 102821.

Griliches, Z. 1979. "Issues in assessing the contribution of research and development to productivity growth." *The Bell Journal of Economics*, 10(1): 92–116.

Haldane, J. B. S. 1956. "Time in biology." *Science Progress*, 44(175): 385–402.

Hansell, M. 2011. "Houses made by portists." *Current Biology*, 21(13): R485–R487.

Harmand, S., Lewis, J. E., Feibel, C. S. et al. 2015. "3.3-million-year-old stone tools from Lomekwi 3, West Turkana, Kenya." *Nature*, 521: 310–315.

Harper, D. A. 2018. "Innovation and institutions from the bottom up: An introduction." *Journal of Institutional Economics*, 14(6): 975–1001.

Hausmann, R., and Hidalgo, C. A. 2011. "The network structure of economic output." *Journal of Economic Growth*, 16: 309–342.

Hausmann, R., Hidalgo, C. A., Bustos, S. et al. 2013. *The Atlas of Economic Complexity*. Massachusetts Institutional Technology Press.

Hayek, F. A. 1948. *Individualism and Economic Order*. Chicago: The University of Chicago Press.

Hayek, F. A. 1952. *The Sensory Order*. Chicago: The University of Chicago Press.

Henrich, J. 2016. *The Secret of Our Success*. Princeton, NJ: Princeton University Press.

Henrich, J. 2020. *The WEIRDest People in the World: How the West Became Psychologically Peculiar and Particularly Prosperous*. New York: Farrar, Straus and Giroux.

Hidalgo, C. A., Klinger, B., Barabási, A. L., Hausmann, R. 2007. "The product space conditions the development of nations." *Science*, 317: 482–487.

Heron-Allen, E. 1915. "A short statement upon the theory, and the phenomena of purpose and intelligence exhibited by the protozoa, as illustrated by selection and behaviour in the forminnifera." *Journal of Microscopy*, 35(6): 547–557.

Hodgson, G. 2007. "The revival of Veblenian institutional economics." *Journal of Economic Issues*, 41(2): 324–340.

Hodgson, G., and Knudsen, T. 2010. *Darwin's Conjecture: The Search for General Principles of Social and Economic Evolution*. Chicago: The University of Chicago Press.

Hordijk, W., and Steel, M. 2017. "Chasing the tail: The emergence of autocatalytic networks." *BioSystems*, 152:1–10.

Howie, J. 1986. "Penicillin: 1929–1940." *British Medical Journal* (Clinical Research Edition), 293(6540): 158–159.

Hublin, J.-J., et al. 2017. "New fossils from Jebel Irhoud, Morocco and the pan-African origin of *Homo sapiens*." *Nature*, 546: 289–292.

Hughes-Hallett, A., Mayer, E. K., Marcus, H. J. et al. 2014. "Quantifying innovation in surgery." *Annals of Surgery*, 260: 205–211. DOI: https://doi.org/10.1097/SLA.0000000000000662.

Hull, N. E. H. 1991. "Networks & bricolage: A prolegomenon to a history of twentieth-century American academic jurisprudence." *The American Journal of Legal History*, 35(3): 307–322.

Hutchinson, G. E. (1957). "Concluding remarks." *Cold Spring Harbor Symposia on Quantitative Biology*, 22: 415–427.

Jacob, F. 1977. "Evolution and tinkering." *Science*, 196: 1161–1166.

Jacobs, J. 2000. *The Nature of Economies*. New York: Vintage Books.

James, W. 1890. *The Principles of Psychology*, volume 2. New York: Henry Holt and Company.

Jones, C. I. 2001. "Was an industrial revolution inevitable? Economic growth over the very long run." *Advances in Macroeconomics*, 1: 1–43.

Jones, C. I., and Romer, P. M. 2010. "The new Kaldor facts: Ideas, institutions, population, and human capital." *American Economic Journal: Macroeconomics*, 2: 224–245.

Joy, J. B. 2013. "Symbiosis catalyses niche expansion and diversification." *Proceedings of the Royal Society of London. Series B, Biological Sciences*, 280: 20122820.

Kahneman, D. 2003. "Maps of bounded rationality: Psychology for behavioral economics." *American Economic Review*, 93(5): 1449–1475.

Kallis, G., Kostakis, V., Lange, S. et al. 2018. "Research on degrowth." *Annual Review of Environment and Resources*, 43: 291–316.

Kant, I. 1787 [1934]. *Critique of Pure Reason*. New York: E. P. Dutton & Co.

Kantorovich, A. 1993. *Scientific Discovery: Logic and Tinkering*. Albany, NY: State University of New York Press.

Kauffman, S. 1986. "Autocatalytic sets of proteins." *Journal of Theoretical Biology*, 119(1): 1–24.

Kauffman, S. 1988. "The evolution of Economic Webs." In P. W. Anderson and K. J. Arrow (eds.), *The Economy as an Evolving Complex System*, volume 5. A Proceedings volume in the Santa Fe Institute Studies in the Sciences of Complexity. New York: Addison-Wesley.

Kauffman, S. 1993. *The Origins of Order*. New York: Oxford University Press.

Kauffman, S. 2000. *Investigations*. New York: Oxford University Press.

Kauffman, S. 2008. *Reinventing the Sacred*. New York: Basic Books.

Kauffman S. 2016. *Humanity in a Creative Universe*. New York: Oxford University Press.

Kauffman, S. 2019. *A World beyond Physics*. New York: Oxford University Press.

Kauffman S., and Roli, A. 2021a. "The world is not a theorem." *Entropy*, 23(11): 1467.

Kauffman, S., and Roli, A. 2021b. "The third transition in science: Beyond Newton and quantum mechanics – A statistical mechanics of emergence." Unpublished manuscript.

Kirzner, I. M. 1973. *Competition and Entrepreneurship*. Chicago: The University of Chicago Press.

Kirzner, I. M. 1982. "Uncertainty, discovery, and human action: A study of the entrepreneurial profile in the Misesian system." In I. Kirzner (ed.), *Method, Process and Austrian Economics*. New York: Lexington Books, pp. 139–161.

Kirzner, I. M. 1997. "Entrepreneurial discovery and the competitive market process: An Austrian approach." *Journal of Economic Literature* 35: 60–85.

Kline, M. A., and Boyd, R. 2010. "Population size predicts technological complexity in Oceania." *Proceedings of the Royal Society of London. Series B, Biological Sciences*, 277: 2559–2564.

Knorr, K. D. 1979. "Tinkering toward success: Prelude to a theory of scientific practice." *Theory and Society*, 8(3): 347–376.

Koppl, R. 2018. *Expert Failure*. Cambridge: Cambridge University Press.

Koppl, R. 2021. "Against expertism." *Review of Behavioral Economics*, 8: 361–377.

Koppl, R., Kauffman, S., Felin, T., and Longo, G. 2015. "Economics for a Creative World." *Journal of Institutional Economics*, 11(1): 1–31.

Koppl, R., and Minniti, M. 2010. "Market processes and entrepreneurial studies." In Z. J. Acs and D. B. Audretsch (eds.), *Handbook of Entrepreneurial Research*, revised edition. Springer.

Koyama, M., and Rubin, J. 2022. *How the World Became Rich: The Historical Origins of Economic Growth*. John Wiley & Sons.

Kremer, M. 1993. Population growth and technological change: One million B. C. to 1990. *Quarterly Journal of Economics*, 108: 681–716.

Kropotkin, P. 1902. *Mutual Aid: A Factor of Evolution*. New York: McClure Phillips & Co.

Kuhn, S. L. 2016. Comment on "Early evidence for brilliant ritualized display." *Current Anthropology*, 57(3): 303–304.

Law, J. 1705 [1966]. *Money and Trade Considered, with a Proposal for Supplying the Nation with Money.* New York: Augustus M. Kelley Publishers.

Lax, E. 2005. *The Mold in Dr. Florey's Coat.* New York: Henry Holt.

Leader, G. M., Kuman, K., Gibbon, R. J., and Granger, D. E. 2018. "Early Acheulean organised core knapping strategies ca. 1.3 Ma at Rietputs 15, Northern Cape Province, South Africa." *Quaternary International,* 480: 16–28.

Levi-Strauss, C. 1966. *The Savage Mind.* Chicago: The University of Chicago Press.

Levine, J. M., and HilleRisLambers, J. 2009. "The importance of niches for the maintenance of species diversity." *Nature,* 461(7261): 254–257.

Lewis, J. E. and Harmand, S. 2016. "An earlier origin for stone tool making: Implications for cognitive evolution and the transition to *Homo,*" *Philosophical Transactions of the Royal Society B: Biological Sciences,* 371: 20150233.

Lotka, A. J. 1926. "The frequency distribution of scientific productivity." *Journal of the Washington Academy of Sciences,* 16: 317–323.

Lowery, Y., and Baumol, W. J. 2013. "Rapid invention, slow industrialization, and the absent innovative entrepreneur in medieval China." *Proceedings of the American Philosophical Society,* 157: 1–21.

Lucas, R. E. 2009. "Ideas and growth." *Economica,* 76: 1–19.

Maddison Project. n.d. "Maddison Historical Statistics." www.rug.nl/ggdc/his toricaldevelopment/maddison/.

Malanima, P. 2011. "The long decline of a leading economy: GDP in central and northern Italy, 1300–1913." *European Review of Economic History,* 15: 169–219.

Mandeville, B. 1729 [1924]. *The Fable of the Bees: Or, Private Vices, Publick Benefits, with a Commentary Critical, Historical, and Explanatory by F. B. Kaye,* in two volumes. Oxford: Clarendon Press.

Marwick, B. 2003. "Pleistocene exchange networks as evidence for the evolution of language." *Cambridge Archaeological Journal,* 13: 67–81.

Marx, K. 1867 [1909]. *Capital: A Critique of Political Economy, volume 1.* Translated by Samuel Morse and Edward Aveling. Chicago: Charles H. Kerr & Company.

Matutinović, I. 2002. "Organizational patterns of economies: An ecological perspective." *Ecological Economics,* 40(3): 421–440.

Maynard-Smith, J., and Harper, D. 2003. *Animal Signals.* Oxford: Oxford University Press.

McBrearty, S., and Brooks, A. S. 2000. "The revolution that wasn't: A new interpretation of the origin of modern human behavior." *Journal of Human Evolution,* 39: 453–563.

McBride, R., and Wuebker, R. 2022. "Social objectivity and entrepreneurial opportunities." *Academy of Management Review*, 47(1): 75–92.

McCloskey, D. N. 2006. *The Bourgeois Virtues: Ethics for an Age of Commerce.* Chicago: The University of Chicago Press.

McCloskey, D. N. 2010. *Bourgeois Dignity: Why Economics Can't Explain the Modern World.* Chicago: The University of Chicago Press.

McCloskey, D. N. 2016. *Bourgeois Equality: How Ideas, Not Capital or Institutions, Enriched the World.* Chicago: The University of Chicago Press.

McMullen, J. S., and Shepherd, D. A. 2006. "Entrepreneurial action and the role of uncertainty in the theory of the entrepreneur." *Academy of Management Review*, 31(1): 132–152.

McPherron, S. P., Alemseged, Z., Marean, C. W. et al. 2010. "Evidence for stone-tool-assisted consumption of animal tissues before 3.39 million years ago at Dikika, Ethiopia." *Nature*, 466: 857–860.

Melchionna, M. A., Mondonaro, A., Serio, C. et al. 2020. "Macroevolutionary trends of brain mass in primates." *Biological Journal of the Linnean Society*, 129: 14–25.

Menger, C. 1871 [1981]. *Principles of Economics.* Translated by James Dingwell and Bert F. Hoselitz. New York: New York University Press.

Mesoudi, A., and Thornton, A. 2018. "What is cumulative cultural evolution?" *Proceedings of the Royal Society B*, 285: 20180712.

Meyer, P. N. 2014. "Shaping your legal storytelling: Voice and perspective can affect how the law is applied to the facts of your case." *ABA Journal*, 100(10): 26–27.

Migliano, A. B., and Vinicius, L. 2021. "The origins of human cumulative culture: From the foraging niche to collective intelligence." *Philosophical Transactions of the Royal Society B: Biological Sciences*, 377: 20200317.

Mises, L. von. 1949. *Human Action: A Treatise on Economics.* New Haven, CT: Yale University Press.

Mitzenmacher, M. 2003. "A brief history of generative models for power law and lognormal distributions." *Internet Mathematics*, 1(2): 226–251.

Mokyr, J. 2005. "Hockey-stick economics: Robert Fogel, 'The Escape from Hunger and Premature Death, 1700–2100'." *Technology and Culture*, 46(3): pp. 613–617.

Muthukrishna, M., and Henrich, J. 2016. "Innovation in the collective brain." *Philosophical Transactions of the Royal Society B: Biological Sciences*, 371 (1690): 20150192. DOI: https://doi.org/10.1098/rstb.2015.0192.

Nelson, K., and Nelson, R. R. 2002. "On the nature and evolution of human know-how." *Research Policy*, 31: 719–733.

Nelson, R. R. 2008. "Bounded rationality, cognitive maps, and trial and error learning." *Journal of Economic Behavior and Organization*, 67: 78–89.

Nelson, R. R., and Winter, S. G. 1982. *An Evolutionary Theory of Economic Change*. Cambridge, MA: Harvard University Press.

Nooteboom, B., Van Haverbeke, W., Duysters, G., Gilsing, V., and van den Oord, A. 2007. "Optimal cognitive distance and absorptive capacity." *Research Policy*, 36: 1016–1034.

Norris, K. S. 1993. *Dolphin Days: The Life and Times of the Spinner Dolphin*. New York: W. W. Norton & Company.

North, D. C., and Weingast, B. R. 1989. "Constitutions and commitment: The evolution of institutions governing public choice in seventeenth-century England." *The Journal of Economic History*, 49(4): 803–832.

Odling-Smee, F. J., Laland, K. N., and Feldman, M. 1996. "Niche construction." *The American Naturalist*, 147(4): 641–648.

Odling-Smee, F. J., Laland, K. N., and Feldman, M. 2003. *Niche Construction: The Neglected Process in Evolution*. Princeton, NJ: Princeton University Press.

Ogburn, W. F. 1922. *Social Change with Respect to Culture and Original Nature*. New York: B. W. Huebsch, Inc.

Oswalt, W. H. 1976. *An Anthropological Analysis of Food-Getting Technology*. New York: Wiley Interscience.

Panger, M. A., Brooks, A. S., Richmond, B. G., and Wood, B. 2002. "Older than Oldowan? Rethinking the emergence of hominin tool use." *Evolutionary Anthropology*, 11: 235–245.

Pareto, V. 1896. *Cours d'Economie Politique Professé a L'université de Lausanne*. Lausanne: F. Rouge, Éditeur.

Pearce, E., and Moutsiou, T. 2014. "Using obsidian transfer distances to explore social network maintenance in late Pleistocene hunter–gatherers." *Journal of Anthropological Archaeology*, 36: 12–20.

Perreault, C., Brantingham, P. J., Kuhn, S. L., Wurz, S., and Gao, X. 2013. "Measuring the complexity of lithic technology." *Current Anthropology*, 54 (S8): S397–S406.

Petroski, H. 1992. *The Evolution of Useful Things*. New York: Alfred A. Knopf.

Potts, J. 2000. *The New Evolutionary Microeconomics: Complexity, Competence and Adaptive Behaviour*. Cheltenham: Edward Elgar Publishing.

Potts, R. et al. 2018. "Environmental dynamics during the onset of the Middle Stone Age in eastern Africa." *Science*, 360(6384): 86–90.

Potts, R. et al. 2020. "Increased ecological resource variability during a critical transition in hominin evolution." *Science Advances*, 6: eabc8975.

Ramoglou, S. 2021. "Knowable opportunities in an unknowable future? On the epistemological paradoxes of entrepreneurship theory." *Journal of Business Venturing*, 36: 106090.

Read, D., and Andersson, C. 2019. "Cultural complexity and complexity evolution." *Adaptive Behavior*, DOI: https://doi.org/10.1177/1059712318822298.

Regis, E. 2020. "No one can explain why planes stay in the air." *Scientific American*, February 1, 2020. Accessed on February 29, 2020 at www.scientificamerican.com/article/no-one-can-explain-why-planes-stay-in-the-air/.

Richardson, G. B. 1960. *Information and Investment: A Study in the Working of the Competitive Economy*. Oxford: Oxford University Press.

Richardson, G. B. 2003. Differentiation and continuity in the market economy. *Advances in Austrian Economics*, 6: 93–99,

Ridley, M. 2020. *How Innovation Works: And Why It Flourishes in Freedom*. New York: Harper.

Rizzo, M. J., and Whitman, G. 2020. *Escaping Paternalism: Rationality, Behavioral Economics, and Public Policy*. Cambridge University Press.

Roli, A., and Kauffman, S. A. 2020. "Emergence of organisms." *Entropy*, 22: 1163.

Romer, P. 1990. "Endogenous technological change." *Journal of Political Economy*, 98(5, part 2): S71–S102.

Rubin, P. 2019. *The Capitalism Paradox: How Cooperation Enables Free Market Competition*. Nashville: Post Hill Press.

Schlebusch, C. M. et al. 2017. "Southern African ancient genomes estimate modern human divergence to 350,000 to 260,000 years ago." *Science*, 358: 652–655.

Schumpeter, J. A. 1911 [1934]. *The Theory of Economic Development*. Oxford: Oxford University Press.

Schurman, J. G. 1887. *The Ethical Import of Darwinism*. New York: Charles Scribner's Sons.

Shackle, G. L. S. 1979. *Imagination and the Nature of Choice*. Edinburgh: Edinburgh University Press.

Shane, S., and Venkataraman, S. 2000. "The promise of entrepreneurship as a field of research." *Academy of Management Review*, 25(1): 217–226.

Shea, J. J. 2003. "The Middle Paleolithic of the East Mediterranean Levant." *Journal of World Prehistory*, 17(4): 313–394.

Shimelmitz, R., and Kuhn, S. L. 2018. "The toolkit in the core: There is more to Levallois production than predetermination." *Quaternary International*, 464: 81–91.

Shipton, C., and Nielson, M. 2018. "The acquisition of biface knapping skill in the Acheulean." In L. D. Di Paolo, F. Di Vincnzo, and F. De Petrillo (eds.), *Evolution of Primate Social Cognition*. Springer, pp. 283–297.

Silverberg, G., and Verspagen, B. 2005. "A percolation model of innovation in complex technology spaces." *Journal of Economic Dynamics and Control*, 29: 225–244.

Simon, H. A. 1955a. "On a class of skew distribution functions." *Biometrika* 42 (3/4): 425–440.

Simon, H. A. 1955b. "A behavioral model of rational choice." *The Quarterly Journal of Economics*, 69(1): 99–118.

Singels, E., and Schoville, B. J. 2018. "A stab in the dark: Testing the efficacy of *Watsonia* exudate as glue for stone tool hafting." *South African Archaeological Bulletin*, 73(208): 147–153.

Smith, A. [1776] 1981. *An Inquiry into the Nature and Causes of the Wealth of Nations*. Indianapolis: Liberty Fund.

Smith, H. N. 2020. "Rock music: The sounds of flintknapping." MA thesis, Kent State University. *Lithic Technology*, forthcoming.

Smith, H. N., Perrone, A., Wilson, M. et al. 2021. "Rock music: An auditory assessment of knapping." *Lithic Technology*, 46(4): 320–335.

Smith, V. 2009. *Rationality in Economics: Constructivist and Ecological Forms*. Cambridge: Cambridge University Press.

Solé, R. V., Armor, D. R., and Valverde, S. 2016. "On singularities and black holes in combination-driven models of technological innovation networks." *PloS One*, 11(1): e0146180.

Solé, R. V., Ferrer-Cancho, R., Montoya, J. M., and Valverde, S. 2003. "Selection, tinkering, and emergence in complex networks: Crossing the land of tinkering." *Complexity*, 8(1): 20–33.

Stark, R. 2005. *The Victory of Reason: How Christianity Led to Freedom, Capitalism, and Western Success*. New York: Random House.

Steel, M., Hordijk, W., and Kauffman, S. 2020. "Dynamics of a birth-death process based on combinatorial innovation." *Journal of Theoretical Biology*, 491: 110187.

Stern, W. 1938. *General Psychology from the Personalistic Standpoint*. New York: The Macmillan Company.

Strandburg, K. J., Csárdi, G., Tobochnik, J., Érdi, P., and Zalányi, L. 2006. "Law and the science of networks: An overview and an application to the 'patent explosion.'" *Berkley Technology Law Journal*, 21(4): 1293–1362.

Tiger, L., and Fox, R. 1966. "The zoological perspective in social science." *Man*, New Series 1(1): 75–81.

Timmer, A. 2015. "Judging stereotypes: What the European Court of Human Rights can borrow from American and Canadian equal protection law." *The American Journal of Comparative Law*, 63(1): 239–284.

Toyota. n.d. "How many parts is each car made of?" Accessed May 29, 2021 at www.toyota.co.jp/en/kids/faq/d/01/04/#:~:text=A%20single%20car%20has %20about,materials%20and%20different%20manufacturing%20processes.

Tryon, C. A., McBrearty, S., and Texier, P.-J. 2005. "Levallois lithic technology from the Kapthurin Formation, Kenya: Acheulian origin and Middle Stone Age diversity." *African Archaeological Review*, 22(4): 199–229.

Tullock, G. 1966 [2005]. *The Organization of Inquiry*. Indianapolis: Liberty Fund, Inc.

Uexküll, J. von. 1934 [2010]. *A Foray into the Worlds of Animals and Humans, with a Theory of Meaning*. Translated by Joseph D. O'Neil. Minneapolis: University of Minesota Press. Translation of *Streifzüge durch die Umwelten von Tieren und Menschen: Ein Bilderbuch unsichtbarer Welten*. Berlin and Heidelberg: Springer.

Ulanowicz, R. E. 1997. *Ecology, the Ascendent Perspective*. New York: Columbia University Press.

Ulanowicz, R. E. 2009. "The dual nature of ecosystem dynamics." *Ecological Modelling*, 220: 1886–1892.

Unattributed. 1920. "Milestones in the development of the American passenger locomotive." *Scientific American*, 123(14): 329n.

Unattributed. 1921. "Past and present of American railroading." *Scientific American*, 125(6): 99.

United States Department of Agriculture (USDA). 2005. *How to Keep Beavers from Plugging Culverts*.

Valverde, S. 2016. "Major transitions in information technology." *Philosophical Transactions of the Royal Society B*, 371: 20150450.

Valverde, S., Solé, R. V., Bedau, M. A., and Packard, N. 2007. "Topology and evolution of technology innovation networks." *Physical Review E*, 76: 056118.

Veblen, T. 1898. "Why is economics not an evolutionary science?" *The Quarterly Journal of Economics*, 12(4): 373–397.

Villmoare, B., Kimbel, W. H., Seyoum, C. et al. 2015. "Early Homo at 2.8 Ma from Ledi-Geraru, Afar, Ethiopia." *Science*, 347(6228): 1352–1355.

Wadley, L. 2016. "Technological transformations imply cultural transformations and complex cognition." In M. N. Haidle, N. J. Conard, and M. Bolus (eds.), *The Nature of Culture: Based on an Interdisciplinary Symposium "The Nature of Culture," Tübingen, Germany*. Dordrecht: Springer, pp. 57–63.

Wadley, L. 2021. "What stimulated rapid, cumulative innovation after 100,000 years ago?" *Journal of Archaeological Method*, 28: 120–141.

Wadley, L., Williamson, B., and Lombard, M. 2004. "Ochre in hafting in Middle Stone Age southern Africa: A practical role." *Antiquity*, 78(301): 661–675.

Watts, I., Chazan, M., and Wilkins, J. 2016. "Early evidence for brilliant ritualized display." *Current Anthropology*, 57(3): 287–301.

Weber, M. 1920 [1992]. *The Protestant Ethic and the Spirit of Capitalism*. New York: Routledge.

Weber, M. 1927 [1981]. *General Economic History*. New Brunswick, NJ: Transaction Books.

Weick, K. E. 1993. "Organizational redesigns as improvisation." In G. P. Huber and W. H. Glick (eds.), *Organizational Change and Redesign: Ideas and Insights for Improving Performance*. Oxford: Oxford University Press, pp. 346–383.

Weitzman, M. L. 1998. "Recombinant growth." *Quarterly Journal of Economics*, 68(2): 331–360.

Welker, B. H. 2017. *The History of Our Tribe: Hominini*. Geneseo, NY: Open SUNY Textbooks.

Wilkins, J. 2020. "Archaeological evidence for human social learning and sociality in the Middle Stone Age of South Africa." In C. Deane-Drummond and A. Fuentes (eds.), *Theology and Evolutionary Anthropology: Dialogues in Wisdom, Humility, and Grace*. New York: Routledge, pp. 119–141.

Wilkins, J., Schoville, B. J., Brown, K. S., and Chazan, M. 2012. "Evidence of early hafted hunting technology." *Science* 338(6109): 942–946.

Williams, H., and Ladhlan, R. F. 2021. "Evidence for cumulative cultural evolution in bird song." *Philosophical Transactions of the Royal Society B*, 377: 20200322.

Wilsson, L. 1971. "Observations and experiments on the ethology of the European beaver (*Castor fiber L.*): A study in the development of phylogenetically adapted behaviour in a highly specialized mammal." *Viltrevy*, 8(3): 117–261.

Witt, U. 2009. "Propositions about novelty." *Journal of Economic Behavior and Organization*, 70: 311–320.

Wolpert, D. H. 2008. "Physical limits of inference." *Physica D: Nonlinear Phenomena*, 237(9): 1257–1281.

Wolpert, D. H. 2017. "Constraints on physical reality arising from a formalization of knowledge." *arXiv preprint arXiv:1711.03499*.

Wrangham, R., and Carmody, R. 2010. "Human adaptation to the control of fire." *Evolutionary Anthropology*, 19: 187–199.

Wreschner, E., Bolten, R., Butzer, K. W. et al. 1980. "Red ochre and human evolution: A case for discussion [and comments and reply]." *Current Anthropology*, 21(5): 621–644.

Young, A. A. 1928. "Increasing returns and economic progress." *The Economic Journal*, 38(152): 527–542.

van Zanden, J. L., and van Leeuwen, B. 2012. "Persistent but not consistent: The growth of national income in Holland 1347–1807." *Explorations in Economic History*, 49: 119–130.

Zipf, G. 1932. *Selective Studies and the Principle of Relative Frequency in Language*. Cambridge, MA: Harvard University Press.

Zipkin, A., Wagner, M., McGrath, K., Brook, A. S., and Lucas, P. W. 2014. "An experimental study of hafting adhesives and the implications for compound tool technology." *PLoS One*, 9(11): e112560.

Acknowledgments

For helpful conversations and guidance, we thank Brian Arthur, Pontus Braunerhjelm, William Butos, Robin Dunbar, Maryann Feldman, April Franco, Sonia Harmand, David Harper, Tim Kohler, Anita McGahan, Andrea Migliano, Richard Nelson, Simon Parker, Mario Rizzo, the late J. Barkley Rosser, Marina Rosser, Mark Sanders, Christian Schade, Ricard Solé, and Jayne Wilkins. Those helpful comments do not imply agreement or relieve the authors of responsibility for any errors in this Element. We thank two anonymous referees for unusually helpful comments. Koppl thanks Syracuse University's Whitman School of Management for financial support. Valverde and Kauffman thank the Complex Systems Lab members for fruitful discussions. Valverde is supported by the Spanish Ministry of Science and Innovation through the State Research Agency (AEI), grant PID2020-117822GB- I00/AEI/10.13039/501100011033.

To tinkering apes everywhere.

Cambridge Elements ☰

Evolutionary Economics

John Foster
University of Queensland

John Foster is Emeritus Professor of Economics and former Head of the School of Economics at the University of Queensland, Brisbane. He is Fellow of the Academy of Social Science in Australia, Life member of Clare Hall College, Cambridge and Past President of the International J.A. Schumpeter Society.

Jason Potts
RMIT University

Jason Potts is Professor of Economics at RMIT University, Melbourne. He is also an Adjunct Fellow at the Institute of Public Affairs. His research interests include technological change, economics of innovation, and economics of cities. He was the winner of the 2000 International Joseph A. Schumpeter Prize and has published over 60 articles and six books.

Isabel Almudi
University of Zaragoza

Isabel Almudi is Professor of Economics at the University of Zaragoza, Spain, where she also belongs to the Instituto de Biocomputación y Física de Sistemas Complejos. She has been Visiting Fellow at the European University Institute, Columbia University and RMIT University. Her research fields are evolutionary economics, innovation studies, environmental economics and dynamic systems.

Francisco Fatas-Villafranca
University of Zaragoza

Francisco Fatas-Villafranca is Professor of Economics at the University of Zaragoza, Spain. He has been Visiting Scholar at Columbia University and Visiting Researcher at the University of Manchester. His research focuses on economic theory and quantitative methods in the social sciences, with special interest in evolutionary economics.

David A. Harper
New York University

David A. Harper is Clinical Professor of Economics and Co-Director of the Program on the Foundations of the Market Economy at New York University. His research interests span institutional economics, Austrian economics and evolutionary economics. He has written two books and has published extensively in academic journals. He was formerly Chief Analyst and Manager at the New Zealand Treasury.

About the Series

Cambridge Elements of Evolutionary Economics provides authoritative and up-to-date reviews of core topics and recent developments in the field. It includes state-of-the-art contributions on all areas in the field. The series is broadly concerned with questions of dynamics and change, with a particular focus on processes of entrepreneurship and innovation, industrial and institutional dynamics, and on patterns of economic growth and development.

Cambridge Elements ≡

Evolutionary Economics

Elements in the Series

A Reconsideration of the Theory of Non-Linear Scale Effects: The Sources of Varying Returns to, and Economics of, Scale
Richard G. Lipsey

Evolutionary Economics: Its Nature and Future
Geoffrey M. Hodgson

Coevolution in Economic Systems
Isabel Almudi and Francisco Fatas-Villafranca

Industrial Policy: The Coevolution of Public and Private Sources of Finance for Important Emerging and Evolving Technologies
Kenneth I. Carlaw and Richard G. Lipsey

Explaining Technology
Roger Koppl, Roberto Cazzolla Gatti, Abigail Devereaux, Brian D. Fath, James Herriot, Wim Hordijk, Stuart Kauffman, Robert E. Ulanowicz and Sergi Valverde

A full series listing is available at: www.cambridge.org/EEVE

Printed in the United States
by Baker & Taylor Publisher Services